YOU ARE
NOT ALONE

YOU ARE NOT ALONE
What Every Woman Needs to Know to Take Financial Care of Herself
Throughout Her Retirement

ISBN: 978-1-956220-59-9

Expert
Press
www.ExpertPress.net

Editing by Tamma Ford
Copyediting by Lori Price
Proofreading by Heather Dubnick
Text design and composition by Emily Fritz
Cover design by Casey Fritz

YOU ARE NOT ALONE

**What Every Woman Needs to Know to Take Financial
Care of Herself Throughout Her Retirement**

Jordyn Richardson

CONTENTS

INTRODUCTION

"It's not how old you are. It's how prepared you are."

The first statement is why I want to encourage all women to read this book! No matter how old you are right now, as soon as you are old enough to have a job or even make even a simple purchase, you are living in a "pay to play" world. Money is involved in all kinds of transactions.

Another reason I am writing this book is because life is unpredictable, and it's important to be prepared as best you can. Though we all know life is not only about money, you need to understand it, be willing to earn and manage your own money, be comfortable talking about financial matters, and plan ahead with loved ones and professionals. That comes home more dramatically for women who are nearing retirement or are already retired when they take an honest look at their financial security for their later years.

In our lobby, you will find a large-scale model of the *Titanic*. It's a symbol that represents the people of the maiden voyage who thought it was an unsinkable ship. Just like your journey into retirement, you need to be on the lookout for icebergs that can sink your retirement. Those icebergs are **never-ending fees and losses**. It's my job to make sure you steer clear of these icebergs in retirement.

Most of us are at ease talking about plans for happy events, like a new baby or a child's wedding. We clam up, though, when deciding on a strategy for the unpleasantness of life, like a major illness or widowhood. We try to convince ourselves they may never happen or will only happen decades from now, so why worry?

It's not about how old you are. It is not about who you are married to or not married to.

> **It is never too soon to prepare yourself and develop financial peace of mind. But it is also never too late to ask for help.**

This book is designed to help you navigate the financial difficulties awaiting you in your golden years. In the following pages, you'll find countless tips and food for thought designed to protect your assets and keep them available for you and your loved ones.

But before I get to that, I need to tell you about what became a legacy for my family. This book begins on a personal note as I introduce you to a woman I know very well—my maternal grandmother, Helen Yuerhs. You'll see in a few pages how she came to provide our family with a valuable legacy (and no, she didn't leave us her huge fortune!).

Helen served as a nurse in World War II. She was a captain, but she never saw active duty. Helen served in Alaska, where she met a young sergeant named Ormond, who happened to be from the same area of Milwaukee she was. To avoid getting caught for fraternization between officers, they snuck around together. After the war, my grandparents got married.

That period of her life was so significant that when she later developed dementia, she began to believe she was going away to serve again. She would often say, "If I knew I wasn't going to see my parents again, I never would have left home." In her mind, at that point, she was an eighteen-year-old nursing student away from home for the first time. I can remember her reporting to my father as if he were the hospital administrator—making reports, telling him about her rounds, and just believing she was, in fact, in a hospital again taking care of patients.

After the war, Helen and Ormond moved to Syracuse, New York, where they settled down and raised their children. Ormond found work doing the accounts for a life insurance firm. Helen remained a nurse until she retired. They lived in the same house in Syracuse for the rest of Ormond's life. In that house, my grandparents raised their five children, including their youngest, my mom, Cathy.

Helen was an incredible woman with a great story to tell, but for our purposes, her story really begins after she and Ormond were well into their retirement years. At that time, my family lived in Elizabethtown, Pennsylvania. My mom was driving up to the old family house in Syracuse every weekend to take care of her aging parents. Now, that's a five-hour drive each way. The commute was quite a lot to ask from a young woman expecting her first child, but my mom was determined to make it. I've always admired how deeply my mother cares about people; she got that from her own mother.

At some point, after months of commuting, my parents decided to approach my grandparents about moving to Elizabethtown. They sat down with Ormond and suggested that maybe it was time to think about him and Helen moving down to Elizabethtown. My father told me Ormond was as polite as ever and heard him out, but he was noncommittal. They had a pleasant dinner and a nice evening all together.

The next day, my grandfather quietly passed away in his own home. I guess his mind was made up; he wasn't going to Pennsylvania. That was tragic and deeply sad, but unfortunately, my parents couldn't focus on their grief because they had to decide what to do for Helen—right now, with no time to prepare.

You can probably guess by now what choice they made: They went ahead with their plan to move her to Elizabethtown. You'd think having an extra adult around could be handy; under normal circumstances, that would have been true.

Unfortunately, right from the get-go, things were not right with Helen. I don't know if it was the shock of losing Ormond, the shock of moving, or simply that she had been able to hide the signs better when she was in her own home. However, it became clear very quickly that Helen's mental health was not as good as my mom and dad had imagined. She had memory deficits severe enough that my parents couldn't even allow her to make grilled cheese; she had forgotten to turn off the stove. That's why our stove never had any knobs attached.

Very simple tasks became problematic for her. My parents ended up having to watch Helen full time and develop strategies to help her. This new responsibility emerged while they themselves were becoming parents for the first time. Somehow, they managed. Helen lived with us for eight and a half years, and my parents were still able to take care of her and raise three wonderful children. But it wasn't easy.

Helen's condition progressively became more difficult as time went on. If this were a book about how to deal with a person with senile dementia, I could fill up entire volumes full of funny and not-so-funny stories about my grandmother and navigating her memory deficits. For instance, we used to go to Panera after church on Sunday; Panera's very crowded, so you have to sit close together. Helen once reached over to somebody else's plate and helped herself to their lunch while they were sitting there. My dad paid for two families' lunches that day.

Those are moments that make you laugh later, but were hard at the time. It is difficult to watch someone deteriorate in front of you, to lose some of their dignity. This was especially true for someone like Helen, who had so much of it before. It requires you to make some lifestyle changes. Needless to say, we stopped going to restaurants. We stopped going anywhere where she might make those sorts of mistakes. She was, at that point, like a small child; my parents had to watch her and watch out for her constantly.

Life in our home was much the same. We had to turn the lock around in our front door, so we (or rather she) were locked in. To get out of our house, you had to use a key. To enter our home, you could just open the door and walk in. That was to prevent Helen from running away down the street, which she had done before. On one occasion, the police had to bring her back. For my parents, it was like having a fourth child in the house; that's what caring for an elderly family member can look like.

Those who are charged with the care of an elder in this type of scenario must change their whole lives. Even when it's willingly taken on, it's a heavy burden, and the burden is all the heavier when there isn't money available to get the help someone needs.

At that time, my mom and dad didn't have the funds to get regular at-home care for Helen. We certainly didn't have the funds to put her in a facility where the burden of her care could be put on strangers. Helen also didn't have the funds left over for it. She had worked hard and saved well throughout her life, but after five kids, the money was all spent. It would've been a real help if somebody had had the funds to help ease the work of taking care of her, but we didn't know how to get the money together.

Here is why I've spent some ink telling you this family story. It is a very real cautionary tale. And it left us a legacy. Hmm, a legacy? What is that exactly? Most of us think about legacies as cash, or as something else transferred by or received from an ancestor or prede-cessor—and you'd be right.

> Helen left us a very real legacy:
> We got to see firsthand what the future
> can look like for you and your loved
> ones if you don't take the proper steps
> <u>now</u> to prepare for it.

The legacy turned into new services, new knowledge, and new information that The Richardson Group shares with all its clients. We learned firsthand as a family what the ramifications of no preparation or planning can be. We never, ever want this for our clients.

Helen lived another eight years in a nursing home and passed away when she was ninety-four. She lived an incredible life that was full of joyous moments, but the last sixteen years were hard on her and our family.

As it turns out, the money for Helen was available that whole time—as it just might be for you, too. My parents just didn't know it *in time*. After Helen passed away, they found out she qualified for the Aid and Attendance Benefit because of her military service in World War II.

Because of her service, her children—including my mom—would have been entitled to $2,600 a month, which they could've used to pay for Helen's care. For over eight-and-a-half years, they missed out on a $176,000 benefit the government would have paid to help her daughter take care of Helen.

Once they realized what was possible, my parents learned about the Aid and Attendance Benefit and Medicaid planning. They quickly discovered just why we had never heard of these benefits: Many advisors are not interested in learning about something that doesn't make them any money. In our county, there were perhaps only three people who really understood the ins and outs of Medicaid and Aid and Attendance Benefit planning, and my mom and dad were two of them. Because of the lessons we learned from our experience with Helen, we've helped a lot more people through our senior practice. We've shown numerous clients how to use these benefits in their own families to provide care where they weren't otherwise able to do it.

Again, why am I spending so much time on this story? I am starting this book with Helen's story because I want you to know these issues you may be facing right now (or might in your future years) are *personal* to me. My family and I are in this business not to make a fortune, but to help families avoid the struggles we went through with my grandmother. Helen was a wonderful woman, a veteran of our armed forces, a life-long nurse, and a great mother and grandmother. She deserved the very best at the end.

Because of her legacy to us, we want to—and now can—make sure you and your family get the very best. That's the mission of The Richardson Group.

Now that you've gotten to know my grandmother Helen, let me tell you a little about my father. Growing up, I knew he owned a financial services business. Over the years he built this business from zero clients in 1996 to a successful business today with thousands of satisfied clients. He never really talked about work at home, but I could see it required a lot of focused energy to keep a business running. It was during these years that my dad imparted the lessons I have come to understand are essential when working in this field.

As he told me about the services his business provided to people, I thought of Helen. I started to get an emotional sense of what my parents went through to ensure her physical safety and care. That legacy morphed into a big part of our educational focus: We are on a campaign to inform our clients and others about the little-known benefits available to retirees.

I belatedly realized the burden Helen's needs put on my family and my parents' finances since I was so young at the time. I only understood she never meant to be such a burden and none of it was her fault.

Now that I work in this industry, I have discovered that married women—far too often—don't have enough to do with their financial planning or fully understand their marital assets or tax picture. I have learned that men—far too often—don't take planning seriously and believe their ten- or even their twenty-year-old plan is still relevant today.

This means that in a crisis or death scenario, a widow or family member will have to gather the tax information and pay the bills, possibly for the first time. If things happen suddenly—if you die—you're going to put a lot of pressure on your family members.

It is not that your family doesn't want to help you, but as a widow or elder single woman, you might feel anxious about putting that kind of pressure on your family. A lot of the women here who are my clients don't want to feel like a burden. They don't ask for help from their family when or as often as they should; they should feel free and comfortable about asking for help within their family but do not.

What was true for my grandma's generation is still true for many baby boomer women: Women grew up believing it was taboo for them to take care of or have opinions about financial matters and their elder-year needs. Having grown up during the Great Depression, my grandmother, in particular, was always very frugal, but being frugal doesn't always mean that you're money smart. It doesn't mean you know how to save properly and make that saved money grow.

I learned from my father's explanations about his business how we can help educate, plan, and coordinate financial matters to make sure a one time financial crisis or widowhood doesn't end in destitution. Being an independent advisor, an unbiased party, I strive to be the advisor you can trust to help navigate your "new normal" after your spouse passes away or when you have that big hit to your life savings after a stock market crash.

My grandmother was not properly prepared. She did not have the proper knowledge (and as they admitted, neither did my parents at that time). A lightbulb lit up for me. I wanted to be part of helping keep other women from having to live a similar story. I know a lot of people don't want to feel like a burden on their families when they get old.

But "a-wishin' and a-hopin'" is not the same as planning.

> **So, ladies, you need to get educated, personally involved, and be hands-on in planning for today and decades to come.**

It's not the same as learning about money and how to keep it for when you need it, but that would be a good start!

If my grandmother had just been more knowledgeable, better prepared, maybe had better financial planning to set aside an amount of money for emergencies ... well, everything might have been different for her and my parents.

Widowhood and dementia may not necessarily be in the cards for everyone, but life is unpredictable, and anything can happen, suddenly derailing your retirement plans.

In the spring of my senior year of high school, my parents told us that Mom had been diagnosed with stage four colon cancer. As parents will do, in the beginning, they didn't really tell us how severe it was. I heard the words "stage four, but she's getting treatment," but I don't think I knew what "stage four" really meant, much less the implications of cancer treatment.

I did know, however, that cancer was a big, scary deal and life-threatening. I was not unaware, but I was faced with worrisome questions I just didn't want to voice, like, "Is she going to die? Can she even get better? How long is Mom going live?" This was right before I left for college, and sometimes I would feel guilty that I wasn't home. At the time I'm writing this book, she has been on several different forms of chemotherapy and will be for the rest of her life. My mother's cancer is aggressive and without continuous chemo, the cancer will continue to come back with a vengeance.

A diagnosis like this is devastating. Medical emergencies are a leading cause of derailed retirement plans; unfortunately, we cannot prepare for every scenario. Entire families suffer when the financial planning for their active years, their retirement years, or their widowhood is not taken care of properly. This is why it's imperative to take the steps you can to prepare—such as maxing out your 401(k) contributions, teaching your children about the importance of starting retirement planning early, and investing in options that provide safety and growth for your money.

So, right now before turning the page into chapter 1, I invite you to ask yourself a few important questions:

- Has any financial advisor ever shown you how to invest without market risk?

- Has any financial advisor ever shown you how much of your income is at risk if your spouse predeceases you? Have you been told how to replace that lost income?

- Do you completely and fully understand all of the risks associated with your investments when your advisor invests your money?

- Does your advisor understand your risk tolerance, and do they invest your money accordingly?

- How long have you worked with your current advisor? Have you ever felt like it might be time to find a new advisor?

These are important questions to ask yourself. The truth is your advisor may not know much more than you about investing; don't assume just because they have a fancy office and use financial jargon that they actually understand the risks they're taking with your money. If you have any sort of reservations that your current advisor might not be the right fit for you, I invite you to continue reading. As you read through this book, you'll find answers to those questions I've posed, and you'll learn how I can help protect you from the issues my real-life clients and other retirees like yourself have as you enter the retirement phase of your life.

I utilize strategies that allow me to say to you—with complete certainty—that regardless of what the stock market does, you're not going to have any years where you have less money than the year before. You have one hundred percent safety.

I want to make sure you have an income from your retirement savings that will last throughout your lifetime, so there are no scrimping and worrying years ahead. There's nothing worse than living longer than your income. That is not a great recipe for retirement happiness. For as long as you live after running out of money, you will regret the choices you make (or don't make) if that ever comes to pass. There's no doubt about it.

Being financially prepared for the future isn't just about having enough money to live on, though. That's why I also want to make sure you are financially ready should you find yourself with deteriorating health. How can we make sure what happened to my grandma Helen doesn't happen to you and your family? How can we best position you so if that happens to you or your spouse, you have the best resources and the best plan available to pay for those unforeseen circumstances? That's the next step.

Finally, I want to make sure the money you don't consume during your lifetime, the money that you leave behind for your heirs, can be passed in the most tax-efficient manner possible. Of the funds left, I want to make sure your main beneficiary is not going to be the IRS! That means making sure you are paying, even on your current income, the lowest tax rate possible. How can you improve your income situation and, at the same time, decrease the amount of taxes you're paying on that income? This poses a problem for even the smartest people, and I want to solve it with you in the best way.

Every client I've worked with has had the same search in common: security. Each man, woman, or couple who has come to see me has expressed their desire to secure their retirement savings in a manner that gives them a worry-free life. This is what I give my clients. No risk. Not a penny of losses. My clients know this when working with me.

Let's get into it now. You will not be planning alone; together we can ensure your golden years are just that—*golden!*

SECTION 1:
WHAT IT MEANS TO BE CONSERVATIVE

I have always been my own advocate; I don't let people stop me from doing what I believe I should do. A lot of people feel embarrassed or pressured when their peers tell them they're going to fail (or that they don't agree with something they're doing or believe they are just plain wrong), but I have always seemed to know I was on the right path. While this isn't a definitive achievement, I am an independent thinker and able to go against the accepted norm to reach my own goals. I'd like for some of that to rub off on my clients! Some of you are confident in what you have and what you want to do. Some of you are not, and it's not because of a lack of knowledge, but a lack of validation.

While working in the financial planning industry, I have often felt less than my male colleagues. At my very first conference, I asked a question about historic stock-market crash indicators, and the gentleman next to me spun around and said, "Wow! You're a lot smarter than you look." Gee, thanks, buddy.

It is no surprise to me when my female clients feel like their advisor only wants to talk and listen to their husbands. Many of the women I work with came to me because they never liked their financial advisor but continued working with them because their husbands liked the guy. Once the people I'm meeting with realize I'm going to listen to everyone in the room, I can see the light bulb go off in the wife's head—it's not that she doesn't know anything about their finances, it's just that no one ever cared to hear her out.

Regardless of why you're here, I want you to feel at ease asking me and my colleagues all your so-called "dumb questions" because, to me, there are no dumb questions. You can't learn without asking, so go ahead and ask! Don't let embarrassment or anxiety about knowing the right terminologies stop you from asking me questions. I'm here to be your partner and work with you to form a clear path. I'm certainly not going to make the big decisions for you, but I will make sure we have explored all the questions and give you answers so you can make informed decisions.

In this section, I'm going to pull back the curtain on mainstream financial planning in America and tell you all the dirty secrets your advisors hope you never find out. It might make you feel like you've wasted years of "good" planning time with the wrong advisor, but it's never too late to get your retirement planning on the right track. Deciding to leave your advisor can be a difficult decision and shouldn't be taken lightly. But I urge you to take in all that I say in the coming pages, and I'm betting I'll see you in my office once you've finished this book.

CHAPTER 1
CONSERVATIVE EQUALS ZERO

I mentioned wanting to uncover the shortcomings of "mainstream" financial planning, but what does that really mean? What is "mainstream" financial planning?

When I say mainstream financial planning, I'm referring to the chain stores of financial services: Ameriprise, Edward Jones, Charles Schwab, Merrill Lynch, etc. These national companies are easily recognizable and are often where people default to when looking for financial advice. However, these national firms are very limited in the types of products and services they offer to their clients. Advisors at these companies tend to push more aggressive portfolios on their clients because they come with higher fees and commissions paid to the advisor. However, just because these firms make financial planning mainstream and accessible, that doesn't mean they are the best to work with.

A common sentiment I hear from my clients is that their definition of "conservative" does not match their advisor's definition. Time and time again, when I review brokerage account statements with clients, I notice how much they have lost in a particular quarter. Oftentimes I see more than a 10 percent decline in their account value when the market is crashing. "Well, how can that be?" my client says, "I told my advisor I wanted to be conservative, and he said that's what I'm in!" Unfortunately, many advisors do believe a 10 percent loss in account value is conservative when the market is down fourteen percent. That's ridiculous. I believe, and many of you probably do too, that conservative *strictly* means NO losses.

> **I also believe being conservative goes beyond mitigating account losses and risk.**

High account management fees are a major reason why an account doesn't grow as much as it should, and it's a major reason why it loses more than it should. If you're looking to be more conservative, simply changing investment strategies with your broker isn't enough, because you're still being charged ridiculously high fees! I do not charge any fees, nor do the companies I choose to work with. Combine no fees with no losses, and you have the *true* definition of conservative.

Most of the clients I meet with do not even know the full scope of fees their advisor is charging them. I want to share a story about a couple and the ridiculous fees they were charged. We can learn several lessons from it.

I met with a couple who were both approaching retirement. I have met with a number of husband-and-wife teams who were already committed to working with another advisor in our area. The husband and wife in my office that day were there because at least one of them (and you'll easily see which one it was) had concerns about their current financial state and were looking to see if they really were with the right advisor.

The husband (let's call him Roger) was singing his current advisor's praises because of the annual golf tournament the advisor's firm hosts for their wealthier clients. During our meeting, the wife (let's call her Rebecca) expressed how concerned she was with losing money. She was worried about the constant fluctuations in their investment accounts and was absolutely floored when she realized how much in fees they had unknowingly been paying to their advisor. On the other hand, while Roger was somewhat concerned about the market risk hurting their retirement nest egg, he wasn't as upset about the fees. In fact, that aspect didn't seem to bother him whatsoever! You see, in his mind, those fees were worth it to him so long as he got to attend the fancy annual golf tournament many of his friends were also invited to.

I explained to Roger and Rebecca that the reason they were all invited to this golf tournament was the size of their accounts! The couple knew they were paying close to 8 percent in fees to their advisor, but they were not on the same page about what this meant to them. Eight percent in fees is an outrageous amount to pay! To Rebecca, that was money they could be putting toward retirement, bills, and grandchildren's college funds. She even stared her husband down and commented, "Our son's first job out of college is paying him less than we're paying our advisor in fees!" However, her husband didn't take the bait. He believed since they never got an itemized bill for those fees, it was money unseen— money that paid for his golf tournaments and the status that came with them.

During our meeting, Roger turned to Rebecca and told her he understood that their money is at risk in the market. "Sweetheart, *everyone's* money is at risk in the market," he said, "but those golf tournaments just mean so much to me."

Rebecca's face crinkled. *Huh?* She exploded, "All that money for a damn golf tournament?! Not only is all of our money at risk, but we're paying for *his* kid's college education, and for what? GOLF?!" Roger was, finally, stunned.

I, on the other hand, was quietly thrilled. This woman *got it*.

This couple was playing what we might call "double jeopardy": They were paying an exorbitant amount in unnecessary fees each year for a portfolio that could lose 50 percent of its value overnight due to a stock market crash. Given their age, now was no time to throw away hard-earned money that would be crucial to their retirement. Roger and Rebecca simply could not afford to lose their nest egg, nor could they afford the hefty fees for a few rounds of golf.

Roger continued to argue in favor of staying with their advisor, stating how important it was to be part of these golf outings with his friends. I stepped in and, again, tried to explain to him the severity of their situation. Statistically speaking, women outlive their husbands. It's crucial for women's financial goals to be considered, especially when planning for retirement—a retirement that she may have to face on her own! If this couple continued down this path, Rebecca's concerns would never be addressed, and she would have become yet another woman with an advisor who doesn't have *her* best interests at heart.

I asked Roger, *"Are you choosing golf over your wife?"*

Her husband sat there, hands folded, eyes diverted.

"Well, say something! What's the answer?" Rebecca stared daggers at him.

He didn't answer right away, which only caused Rebecca to grow more and more upset. The three of us sat there in silence for about ten minutes before Roger answered. He finally mumbled that his wife was right—they needed to stop the bleeding. I was so glad that Roger finally saw what his wife was seeing, and they were able to make the decision together to discontinue the never-ending fees they were paying and get rid of the risk of losing money.

I wish I could say this was the only couple I've had who didn't see eye to eye regarding their finances. Sadly, this couple was not even in the worst shape I've seen. Do you want this to be your story?

I see a fair number of married men who stubbornly stand their ground, saying, "We're not moving our money. We'll be fine." I've met with many women who came to see me even though their husbands were not interested, and I often never hear from them again because their husbands were also too stubborn to consider a change.

However, for those clients who do leave their advisors to work with us, they all have one search in common: security. That is what I give them. No risk. Not a penny of losses. Our clients know that no matter what happens in the market, their money is safe. The husbands we work with know that if something happens to them,

I will be there to help their wives through the next steps. And most importantly, the women I already work with all know that I'm in their corner to work with them to build the retirement they envision.

CHAPTER 2
FEES ARE HURTING YOU MORE THAN YOU KNOW

In the previous chapter, I mentioned how having account management fees is not my definition of a conservative portfolio. Many of you may agree with me, but also question how much fees *really* impact your overall account balances. So, let's pull back the curtain on how fee structuring works for mainstream, fee-based advisors.

Traditionally, almost every financial planner charges their clients fees. The mainstream advisory firms all charge their clients fees, as do most of your local advisory firms. If you're unsure if your current advisor charges fees, ask yourself if you have any stocks, mutual funds, *variable annuities*, or other investments. If your money is invested in any of these, you're being charged fees.

When it comes to breaking down the clandestine way fee-based advisors make their money, I like to use buying houses as an example. When you buy a house, there are typically three parties involved: you (the buyer), the broker assisting in the sale of the home, and the seller.

> ## When you have found your dream home, what happens?

Well, you (the buyer) pay the cost of the house (the agreed purchase price). The seller pays the broker for their time and effort in procuring the sale via a one-time finder's fee while banking the remainder of the purchase amount you paid. You didn't pay the broker anything, but he is compensated.

But what if we bought houses the same way we let traditional fee-based advisors manage our money? That would mean, as the buyer, you would pay the broker an upfront fee (while the seller still pays the broker their commission). You would also be required to write the broker a check every year for 2 percent of the value of your home for as long as you live there. That's crazy, right? No one would buy houses following that method. Well, then why would you follow that model when investing?

Fee-based advisors make their money in two ways:

1. By charging their clients a fixed percentage of their portfolio every year

2. By selling investments that pay high
    commissions to the advisor via hidden fees
    straight out of your pocket

The fixed percentage that advisors charge their clients is referred to as the *advisory fee*. Typically, this is the only fee being disclosed to the clients, and it ranges from 1 to 3 percent of your portfolio value. This is the first way advisors make money for themselves.

The second type of fees I mentioned—the hidden ones—I like to call "termites." Termites work secretly on your home's foundation, eating away at the structure until one day the whole thing collapses on you. Just like those termites, these hidden fees are secretly at work in your accounts, eating away at your account value.

If someone else has been managing your money, you may never even know that the termites are there, as *they are never listed on your statements*. Unless you really take the time to inspect and examine your investment statements with a professional like me, you could continue to be a victim of decreased gains due to these fees!

While advisors have to disclose their annual *advisory fees*, the industry currently has no practice in place requiring these advisors to disclose *hidden* fees. I have seen accounts with hidden fees totaling as much as 8 percent—and that didn't even include the advisory fee! On a $500,000 investment account, that means you could

YOU ARE NOT ALONE

be paying as much as $50,000 in fees—*every single year!*
I don't know what *you* would do with an *extra* $50,000
a year, but I have a few ideas of my own that would suit
me just fine! And here's the catch: The advisors don't ever
have to tell you about those fees. Red flag, anyone?

Wall Street Journal

Is Your Financial Advisor in the 'hidden fee' Hall Of Shame?

By **Mitch Tuchman**

Published: November 16, 2017

These seemingly small costs can eat into your retirement savings.

A new report shows that the cost difference between low-fee and high-fee financial advisors is staggering — roughly nine times more costly, mostly hidden in fine print.

That means an account with $100,000 in investment value costs $380 a year to manage, counting both fund fees and face time with an advisor.

Charles Schwab is comparable at 0.44% ($440 a year) and from there prices begin to ramp up. Personal Capital, which did the research, came in at between 0.87% and 0.97%.

Source: https://www.marketwatch.com/story/is-your-financial-adviser-in-the-hidden-fee-hall-of-shame-2017-11-16.

At The Richardson Group, we invest people's money the same way people buy houses. We never charge our clients a fee for working with us. We do not *ever* offer investments that require the client to pay us back a certain percentage each year. Our investments don't come with termites. Just like in the house-buying example, you deposit your money into the investment account, and the "seller" (the company offering the product) pays The Richardson Group a one-time finder's fee *from their own pockets.* It is the product-selling company's compensation to us; your money is never part of that. Our investments also never have any recurring fees! We all know the saying, "Nothing in life is free," but this is about as fee-free as it gets.

In fact, the specific type of licensing my colleagues and I hold forbids us from charging our clients fees and choosing risky investment options. Whereas fee-based financial planners choose to carry financial service licenses that do allow them to carry fees, their licenses also protect them from being sued when they do lose your money! After hearing that, who would you rather work with?

Because The Richardson Group is solely commission-based, 100 percent of the investment money you place with us goes to work for you. Your money can never be lost due to fees or market risk.

CHAPTER 3
RISK IS THE BIGGEST THREAT TO YOUR RETIREMENT

Investment risk is one of the most talked-about topics in the financial planning world. When discussing your risk tolerance with an advisor, many will ask you if you want to be aggressive, moderate, or conservative. The younger you are, the more risk tolerant you may be. However, the closer you are to retirement, the more you want to be conservative with your retirement accounts. Conservative equals no losses. Does your current advisor agree with that?

When working with a mainstream brokerage like Ameriprise, Edward Jones, Raymond James, etc., your accounts are being exposed to stock market risk. Large corporations like this employ people with securities licenses, meaning their advisors are licensed to sell investments that put your hard-earned money directly in the stock market. Sure, advisors with securities licenses are also allowed to sell no-fee, no-loss investments like I sell, but they don't sell these types of products because it pays less. In the last chapter, I talked about how high your account fees are, and it's because the advisors you work with sell stock market investments.

When you invest in the stock market, you will see your accounts grow when the market is rising. But the one thing I see time and time again in people's investment accounts is that their yield does not match the growth in the market. Why is that? It's because of the excessive fees your advisor charges you. When I point out that our clients see the same, if not better, returns without the possibility of any losses or fees, these people quickly turned into clients of mine. To them, the possibility of tremendous growth does not outweigh the guaranteed security I offer them.

Why is it that we women live longer? Our risk tolerance is different from men's. Men typically have a higher tolerance or acceptance of risk than women. Women have an aversion to risk!

Apply this idea to money and retirement management, and you'll deduce that men are less conservative and more apt to make far riskier decisions with their money than women. Have you heard your advisor talk about "a high-growth portfolio"? That high-risk investment is marketed to men "because it has higher returns." Risk-taking men respond well to this type of marketing. Women sit back instead and ask, "How much could I lose if the market crashes?"

It is not only my personal experience but statistically valid that *women make better financial decisions than most men* because of our risk aversion. We make decisions based on information, data, knowledge, and trust. We activate our lie detectors. We read reviews, ask trusted friends and family members for recommendations—and then follow up on those recommendations with more personal research.

> **Seventy percent of widows change financial advisors upon the death of their spouses.[1]**

Many newly widowed and divorced women come into my office because they're ready for a change in advisors and need proper guidance on what to do next. Many of these women tell me their husbands hardly involve them in the finances, making it especially difficult after they've passed to know what to do next. All of these women share the sentiment that their current advisor is too risky, and they come to me, searching for security.

---

1   www.fa-mag.com/news/financial-life-after-widowhood-36922.html

I hope you see now that your needs might not be met due to the wrong selection criteria for a financial advisor. Any advisor has the ability to sell no-fee, no-loss investment options, so why don't they? Because if they don't use risky, stock-market-based investments, those advisors don't make as much money from you. Advisors who collect loads of fees from you do not take any of your needs into account, only their own. Fee-hungry advisors push their clients into making poor financial decisions. That should worry you if your husband is their client!

While I could make ten times the amount I am making, I refuse to put my needs before the needs of my clients. I have no interest in selling risky, fee-ridden products like many advisors do. Just like my clients, I sleep at night knowing that I'm not losing a penny of anyone's money.

SECTION 2:
SAFE MONEY SAVINGS

If you have your retirement savings invested in the stock market, I hope by now you may be reconsidering that choice. If you are approaching retirement or have already retired, I strongly urge you to begin considering other options for your nest egg savings. When you are no longer working and are relying on a fixed income from Social Security and pension payments, you cannot afford to risk your savings to a 30 percent loss due to market risk. You simply do not have the time to make up for a catastrophic loss during your retirement years.

You may agree with me on this but also be questioning what other options you have. When the market has taken a dive, you may hear people say, "Thank goodness I put my money in cash before the crash happened!" But keeping your money in a low-yield interest-bearing savings account is not a long-term solution when you need that money to grow to provide income and keep up with inflation. So, if you can't keep your money in the market and you can't keep it in cash, what can you do?

This is where I come in. As I mentioned before, I only offer no-fee, no-loss accounts, but what exactly is that type of account?

CHAPTER 4
HOW TO BE
SAFE MONEY SMART

In the previous chapters, I spent time covering the major shortfalls of your current advisor: They subject your life savings to risky investments in order to line their pockets with the fees they collect from you. Traditional fee-based advisors do not have your best interests in mind—they simply can't when they're choosing lesser-than products with higher fees and commissions. It is, however, in your best interest to read on to learn how to protect your retirement assets today, tomorrow, and for the rest of your life.

To start off, I want to use a "Tale of Twin Sisters" to illustrate just how damaging market risk can be during your golden retirement years. Two sisters, Sally and Jane, lived very similar lives. They went to the same university, worked in the same industry making similar wages, retired at similar ages, and had similar health concerns. Sally and Jane also retired with similar retirement savings, but the biggest difference is Jane retired in 1990, ten years before Sally did in 2000.

Ten years may not seem like a huge difference, especially today when people are retiring at all different ages, but this was a crucial difference in these sisters' retirement stories.

If we look at the illustration below, we can see just how much a market crash early in retirement can affect you for years to come. When Jane chose to retire in 1990, she didn't know what the market would look like in the coming years. She was lucky that the market didn't crash early on in her retirement. But Sally was not as lucky. As you can see, the first three years of her retirement savings were hit with negative market returns, followed by a devastating market crash in 2008.

What did Sally do wrong here? Nothing, really. Her only mistake was trusting the stock market at the wrong time. Unless she had a crystal ball, Sally had no way of knowing what the market was going to do; nonetheless, she trusted the market at a bad time. And I have bad news for you: You won't know when the market will crash either.

TWO SISTERS TWO (DIFFERENT) RETIREMENTS

- Each has $500,000 saved in their IRAs at retirement.
- Both will use $30,000 annually as income.
- Jane retires in 1990.
- Sally retires in 2000.
- The result?

INCOME AND SEQUENCE OF RETURN

Jane   Retired in 1990

YEAR	RETURN	WD	BALANCE
1990	-4.34%	$30,000	$449,602
1991	20.32%	$30,000	$504,865
1992	4.1%	$30,000	$494,667
1993	13.72%	$30,000	$528,419
1994	2.14%	$30,000	$509,085
1995	33.45%	$30,000	$639,340
1996	26.01%	$30,000	$767,829
1997	22.64%	$30,000	$904,87
1998	16.10%	$30,000	$1,015,728
1999	25.22%	$30,000	$1,234,328

Sally   Retired in 2000

YEAR	RETURN	WD	BALANCE
2000	-6.18%	$30,000	$440,954
2001	-7.10%	$30,000	$381,776
2002	-16.76%	$30,000	$292,819
2003	25.32%	$30,000	$329,364
2004	3.15%	$30,000	$308,794
2005	-0.61%	$30,000	$277,094
2006	16.29%	$30,000	$287,345
2007	6.43%	$30,000	$273,892
2008	-33.84%	$30,000	$161,359
2009	18.82%	$30,000	$156,081

While it's too late for Sally, it's not too late for you. There is a way to avoid having her same unfortunate fate. My strategies allow you to avoid stock market losses, no matter when they happen or how devasting they are. With my no-fee, no-loss strategies—which are called *indexed annuities*—you will never lose a penny because it's impossible to lose money in indexed annuities. You can only ever make money. If Sally had seen me and transferred her retirement savings out of the stock market and into one of my indexed annuities, she would be way ahead of the game—no matter when she retired.

That can be true for you, too. No matter when you retire, no matter if the stock market crashes early on or later in your retirement, you will never have to worry about losing money. Working with me, you will benefit either way. This is that security I've been talking about. Indexed annuities not only protect you when the market is down, but you participate in the growth when the market is up. When I hear people say the only other option to keeping their money in the stock market is putting it in cash, I tell them they're wrong. Indexed annuities *are the other option*. Why wouldn't you want to participate in the growth of the market without any risk of loss?

You and I share the same goal when it comes to your retirement nest egg: protect it as much as possible while making as much as possible. Unlike keeping your money in cash to avoid market risk, indexed annuities offer you the ability to make just as much in your accounts as you would if you were directly invested in the stock market— if not more! No matter how well your brokerage accounts have performed in years past, your gains could always have been higher without the hefty fees your advisor has been charging you. With these annuities, there are no fees! This is why I say your earning potential is possibly even higher with these accounts because there is no possibility of your account growth being decreased by fees and loss.

If you still don't believe me about indexed annuities' potential growth, take a look at the graph below.

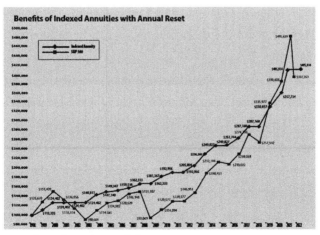

[image 4 – annuity vs market]

In meeting with your advisor, I'm sure you've heard the saying "Buy low, sell high." Sure, that's great advice. But when the market is down and has no intention of turning around anytime soon, you have to get out as fast as possible. There's no time to wait for the market to bounce back when your retirement savings are at risk.

The way you get out is by switching your retirement accounts over to an indexed annuity. Traditional IRAs, Roth IRAs, 401(k)s, 403(b)s, pensions, and even CDs can all be moved into this type of annuity. As soon as you decide to make the switch from high-fee, risky investments to a secure indexed annuity, the losses stop.

The chart above illustrates the difference between investing in the stock market versus an indexed annuity during the same period. Without getting too technical, the chart shows us that an annuity has outperformed the market by avoiding when the stock market dropped. So why, at this point, do you still want to be in the stock market?

Let's break this down. When you invest in an indexed annuity, your money is never subjected to market loss. During an economic recession, that means that you will never lose a penny, and when the market finally bounces back, you start from the top again. As soon as the market turns positive, you start making money again.

Indexed annuities are the safest investment offered. If you recall, I mentioned how your broker has probably asked you about your risk tolerance and given you three options: aggressive, moderate, or conservative. In traditional financial planning, conservative typically means bonds and mutual funds with targeted retirement dates.

Unfortunately, we're in for a double whammy in the coming years as the market declines and interest rates rise. Investment returns are going to be hammered. Bonds are not safe either. And if you're with a traditional fee-based advisor, they won't be able to offer complete and total safety. There will always be fees, and some degree of risk involved when working with a traditional advisor.

What is your **RISK** tolerance?

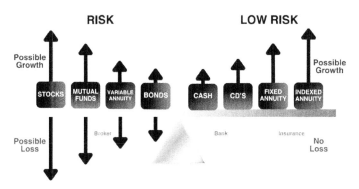

I define conservative investing as ZERO risk tolerance. To me, being conservative with your money means you don't ever want to lose money. In the image above, you can see the various types of investments and how they each relate to growth and risk potential.

Working with a broker who puts your money in stocks, mutual funds, and variable annuities, you're guaranteed loss during a stock market decline. While bonds may be a safer option than those three, they are still at risk of losing value and the growth potential is not as great. Cash, CDs, and *fixed annuities* are more on the conservative end, but their growth potentials are not as high. Indexed annuities are the only investment option that guarantees no loss of value while still providing the same growth potential as the stock market.

I have seen many clients express to their advisors how wary they are of the market. And in each case, their advisor told them to just stick it out. By the time these people come to see me, that bad advice has cost them 10, 20, or even 30 percent in account losses. Your traditional advisor is never going to tell you to get your money out of the market because they don't make money if you do. Even if the market doesn't crash in the coming years, you are still losing money through fees. Not to mention, when your money is invested in the stock market, you don't own the gains in your account. When your gains and deposit are subjected to market risk, they can be lost at any time. You're only renting your gains in the stock market; it's not real money.

However, in an indexed annuity, any interest earned is YOURS. Interest earned can never be lost in an indexed annuity. There's no renting the gains in these annuity accounts—only owning the gains.

With all that risk on your shoulders, you might be thinking you should be sharing that risk exposure, but that's not the case. You're taking on all the risk yourself, but your advisor is benefiting from you even when you are losing money. When we look back at the example of Roger and Rebecca, the couple arguing over the fancy golf tournament, they were being hammered with fees. Even when that couple loses 50 percent in the next stock market crash, their advisor will continue lining his pockets off their misfortune.

> **I want to put your money in a safe place—a place where a negative market doesn't hurt you.**

I don't want you paying never-ending fees, either, which is why I will never charge you a fee, and I'll never put your money in an investment that charges you fees.

You don't have to just take my word for it; plenty of retirement specialists agree with me that indexed annuities are the best option for your retirement accounts. Suze Orman is the first who comes to mind. She has been a huge influence in my life and business. In her book *The Road to Wealth*, Suze suggests that a good indexed annuity may be right for people who don't want to take any risks but still want to play the stock market.

That's you, right? You want to be safe, don't you? You want your retirement to look like Jane's, not Sally's.

Suze further agrees with the fact that indexed annuities "cannot go down" and while it may limit your upside, it "protects you from a downturn."

Tony Robbins, another leading voice in the financial services industry, also agrees with Suze Orman and me that indexed annuities may be the better choice for people entering their golden years. Tony considers indexed annuities a great investment option because they allow for "a great upside" while also providing a "guaranteed lifetime income."[2]

I'm not here to sell you Orman and Robbins products. I believe in indexed annuities so much that I have money invested in them, as well as my parents and grandmother. I would never put my client's money in an investment I wasn't willing to put my grandmother's money in.

In March 2008, my father put his money in an indexed annuity. A year later, the country was in a panic over the 50 percent stock market crash. However, my dad and all of our clients were worry-free. Neither he nor a single one of his clients had lost a penny.

---

2   "How much do I need for retirement?", Team Tony, https://www.tonyrobbins.com/wealth-lifestyle/much-need-retire/

Following that devastating crash were eight years of continued stock market growth. Everyone's accounts were up 98 percent in just nine years if they had money invested with our group from March 2008 to March 2017. All of the money was theirs to keep. Not a penny of earned interest can ever be lost, either. Not a single fee was deducted from their accounts. Who else is offering you a product like this? No one.

During the early spring of 2022, I met with a couple who attended one of my workshops. Let's call them Mary and Ken. They attended because Mary, especially, was feeling ignored by her advisor. She had been worried about the market ever since retiring a few years ago and had expressed this many times to her husband and their advisor. Previously, her husband wasn't too concerned; the market had been doing okay. But after the market started falling from its all-time historical high on January 5, 2022, Ken was also getting concerned and came to the workshop to see if there was another option for them.

When I met with this couple, they brought their most recent account statements, and I saw they were primarily invested in mutual funds and variable annuities. Both of these investments carry high risks and high fees. Their statements showed that from January 1, 2022, to March 31, 2022, they had already lost 15 percent; they had a very aggressive portfolio. After showing Mary and

Ken all the downsides to remaining in the market and the security I could provide them, Mary looked at her husband and said, "Ken, we would be stupid to stay in the market." I agreed. Under my advisement, they knew they wanted to get their money out of mutual funds and the variable annuity as quickly as possible. An indexed annuity was absolutely the best option for them.

Here's the real reason I'm sharing this story with you: As we were in the process of moving their accounts over to the indexed annuity, their broker actually called Mary and Ken and asked what they were doing. They explained how they couldn't afford to lose any more money and that they would be working with me since I could provide the security they were looking for. The broker said, "Well, why didn't you tell me? I can do that for you." Mary chimed in, "I asked you months ago for something safer and here we've lost 15 percent. Why didn't you do it for us then?"

You see, their broker worked for one of those chain brokerages. When he said he could help them, Mary and Ken knew he was lying. Those guys are just not able to offer the products that provide you absolute protection. They are only able to offer certain products, meaning they can only either make you money or make your money safe. They can't do both as I can.

While still making money, this *safe money* concept is the foundation of everything I offer to my clients. I want to make sure your money is secure, safe, and worry-free.

I work with another client, Rose, who I've known for many years. When she first came to see me, she was still working as a secretary for another fee-based financial planning firm (I won't name names here). She was referred to me by her sister, who is also a client.

At first, I could tell Rose was only there to see me to appease her sister. Since she worked at a financial planning office, she thought she knew what was really happening with her accounts. But unfortunately, these companies are very secretive with their practices. Rose told me she wasn't paying any fees since she worked there. I asked her to prove it to me, so she pulled out her statements and proudly exclaimed, "See! It doesn't say anywhere on there I'm being charged a penny to have my money managed."

As I told you previously, most fees are hidden. I showed her how each transaction listed on her page came with a secret fee. Her advisor had her mostly in American Funds, a special type of mutual fund that charges the highest fee out of any other. Each time he bought and sold a mutual fund in her account—which was practically daily—she was incurring three secret fees attached to every mutual fund:

- A 12b-1 mutual fund fee

- An operating fee

- A marketing fee

I also showed her how this company has a standard 1 percent advisor fee they charge every single client. Even though Rose was working there, they legally could not waive that fee—that would be called *rebating*, and it's highly illegal. Registered investment advisors cannot waive a mandatory fee for anyone.

Once Rose realized she was being lied to, she was pretty upset. She had over a million dollars invested that she had accumulated through inheritance and savings. She couldn't believe just how much her colleague was making per year off her account alone. Now that she knew she was in fact paying a fee, she no longer wanted to assume the risk she was taking by having this much money invested in the stock market. She made the decision to work with me and retire early. She was done with her advisor.

Rose has a lot in common with Mary and Ken; they too were being lied to by their advisors. Rose thought she wasn't being charged to have her money managed, and Mary and Ken were told they could have "just asked" for something safer. But it's not true. Advisors like these cannot offer the same things I offer.

For me, it's fantastic that they can't! I have no competition. Safe money strategies are all I use, and no one else can compete with that. Who can complain about making 100 percent on their money in ten years? Remember, every client who worked with my group from 2008 to 2018 DOUBLED their money. *Every single client!* Has your broker done that for you?

I bet not, and I bet other advisors can't explain why, but I can. The answer comes down to one word: *fiduciary*.

Fiduciary Oath

We believe in placing our clients' best interests first. Therefore, we commit to the following five fiduciary principles:

We will always put our clients' interests first.

We will act with prudence; that is, with the skill, care, diligence, and good judgement of a professional.

We will not mislead clients, and will provide conspicuous, full and fair disclosure of all important facts.

We will avoid conflicts of interest.

We will fully disclose and fairly manage, in our clients' favor, any unavoidable conflicts.

_____	_____
Advisor Signature	Date
_____	_____
Advisor Name	Firm Name

Being a fiduciary means I have a legal responsibility to work in my clients' best interests. I've signed the fiduciary oath, so the client's interests always have to come before mine, and I must prove that. For example, unlike your brokers, I have to disclose every conflict of interest I have.

While your brokers are hiding their fees, I cannot and do not hide the fact that I earn a commission. Whenever a client asks me how I make money, I proudly tell them the insurance company compensates me, and I also tell my clients how much I make. I have nothing to hide. Being a fiduciary doesn't just mean I have to disclose conflicts of interest—it also means I have to prove why the products I recommend are in your best interest.

I want to distinguish the difference between "in your best interest" and "suitable for you." As a fiduciary, I will do what is *best* for you. Fee-based advisors will do what is *suitable* for you.

Suitable can mean "just okay." It's not the best option out there, but it isn't a Ponzi scheme. That's what suitable gets you. What's best for you is a contractual guarantee that you will pay no fees and never lose a penny.

At this point, I hope you and are on the same page: it's time to break up with your broker. I understand this is not always an easy task. Maybe your advisor goes to your church or is your husband's golf buddy. Whoever they may be, you cannot be concerned with hurting someone's feelings when it comes to protecting your entire life savings. It's nothing personal—it's just business.

Many people stay with their advisors because they want to avoid conflict and feeling guilty. You should never feel guilty about doing the right thing for yourself and the security of your retirement. I've seen advisors use every trick up their sleeve to retain a client who has expressed the wish to work with someone else. I've had advisors show up at a client's home with dozens of roses. I've seen advisors threaten clients. And I've seen advisors refuse to let their clients move their own money. No matter what an advisor tells you, you're being cheated. This is your money. Don't let someone bully you into continuing to risk it all.

I know firsthand just how intimidating it can be to break up with your broker, which is why I will help you every step of the way. From start to finish, I will navigate the breakup with you. I will call the broker with you; I'm not afraid to tell him what you want to do.

CHAPTER 5
REDUCE YOUR TAX BILL

Avoiding account management fees and staying away from market risk are two major ways to save your money, but taxes are another threat to your retirement assets and income. In this chapter, I'm going to explain all the ways you can help reduce your tax burden, thus putting more money into your pocket every year. Just about every source of income is subject to federal and state income tax. IRA distributions, Social Security payments, pension payments, annuity distributions, inheritance, capital gain income, and interest income are all subject to income taxation. While the easy answer to reducing taxes is to just make less money, that's not going to help you pocket more money. The first step to reducing taxes is by eliminating capital gain "income."

Why did I put quotations around income?

As I mentioned before, when you have a brokerage account where your investments are invested directly in the stock market, any gains applied to your account are not owned by you; they're only being rented. Even though the gains you see in your brokerage accounts are simply being rented by you, they still show up on your tax return as income.

Capital gains are applied anytime you have a profit from the sale of an investment, whether it be a physical property or a mutual fund that you sold. IRAs, 401(k)s, and annuities are all *"tax-deferred,"* meaning you pay no capital gain tax on the money earned in these types of accounts. You defer the taxes and only pay when you withdraw money from the account. But any other accounts are subject to annual capital gains tax.

When you have a non-IRA brokerage account, you will see capital gain, dividend, and interest income appear on your tax return every year. Even if you choose to have your dividends reinvested—meaning you don't receive monthly dividend checks, and instead your dividends are paid directly back into your brokerage account—dividend reinvestment not only costs you a transaction fee, but also costs you in taxes even though you were never paid that money. Capital gain income is another form of phantom income. Capital gain simply refers to how much your account increased in value—it doesn't mean you benefited by receiving any income from it. Yet, you're taxed even if you leave it in the account.

If you look at your annual tax summary from a brokerage account, you may see a long list of transactions. Whenever a stock or mutual fund is sold for a profit, the capital gain is accrued. If your advisor is constantly buying and selling stocks or mutual funds, it's costing you money!

So how can you avoid excessive and unnecessary taxes from dividend and capital gain income? Come to see me and get an indexed annuity. Not only do indexed annuities not charge you any fees and guarantee you can never lose any money, but they also are tax-deferred—meaning you will never pay taxes on your gain unless you take a withdrawal from your account. Isn't that great?

I once worked with a couple who were only clients of our tax preparation business at the time. I had just finished their tax return and was meeting with them to review it. One thing that stood out to me was the fact that over half their income came from capital gains and interest! Other than Social Security, this was all they were earning. Because their capital gains were so high, their Social Security was taxed over 50 percent!

During our meeting, we reviewed the current investments they had with their broker. All of their investable assets were in various mutual funds, which is what was causing the capital gains. I explained how a tax-deferred annuity could seriously help reduce their tax bill to almost zero by eliminating 100 percent of the capital gain and interest income in their accounts. Plus, the annuity would also produce similar annual returns to their current investments. It was a no-brainer for this couple to dump their broker and switch their investments into an annuity.

I've helped many clients reduce income tax bills simply by moving their brokerage accounts into a tax-deferred annuity. And when you reduce capital gain and dividend income, your Social Security check is higher each month, putting more money in your pocket, and less in Uncle Sam's.

If you have savings accounts, CDs, or government-issued I-bonds, you're also being regularly taxed on those accounts. While government bonds give you the option to defer taxes until the end of the term, you are still required to pay taxes on the full amount of the gains. Interest earned in CDs and savings accounts is also taxable each year. Not only are you paying taxes on these accounts, but you are not even earning that much to make the taxes worth it. But what if I told you there was another option to CDs and savings?

Just like indexed annuities, fixed annuities come without fees and risk, but they are typically used for short-term investing. Much like CDs, fixed annuities offer a guaranteed interest rate during an agreed-upon term. Typically, I recommend my clients use three- or five-year fixed annuities instead of CDs. I also recommend that for the average person, having any more than $20,000–$30,000 in savings is too much. Savings accounts hardly pay anything, and keeping any funds beyond your emergency fund in a savings account is just wasting money.

Banks pay very little interest, especially compared to insurance companies. In 2022, most banks were renewing 36-month CDs below 1 percent; meanwhile, insurance companies were issuing three-year fixed annuities above 3.5 percent! On $100,000, investing in a 3.5 percent three-year annuity rather than a 0.75 percent 36-month CD is a difference of over $8,500! And any money in the fixed annuity is not taxed unless you take it out; at the end of the three years, you can renew the contract and still not pay any taxes. Why settle for less than half the interest and a tax bill when you can infinitely compound your money with fixed annuities?

> **Compared to indexed annuities, fixed annuities are just as safe and have many of the same key benefits.**

However, indexed annuities offer much higher earning potential than fixed annuities, which is why

I typically only recommend fixed annuities for short-term investing. If you have an abundance of savings or like the flexibility of CDs, fixed annuities are perfect for you. At the end of the short annuity term, the money is completely liquid. If you're thinking of moving in a few years and know you'll need that extra $100,000 in your savings account, the fixed annuity is perfect.

CHAPTER 6
AVOID THE SURVIVING SPOUSE INCOME GAP

Many people can accept everything I've written in this book so far as true, yet still insist they don't need help. I find the people who think they know it all are the ones who need the most guidance.

I met such a couple, whom I'll call Betty and Joe, at one of the very first workshops I led. After I had finished presenting, they came up to me and expressed how glad they were that they came and how excited they were about all they had learned from me. Betty and Joe rattled off some questions; typically I'd respond that such in-depth questions would require making an appointment with me so I could really explore their situation and give them the best answers. But they were going to Florida for the winter in a week and couldn't wait to have these questions answered.

I like to help people, and even though I wasn't sure if I'd hear from this couple again after answering their questions, it didn't matter—if I could help them then and there, I would. Joe explained their finances, telling me the types of accounts they had and the estimated values of each. Most of the questions they had were easily answered, many relating to IRA rules. Then they expressed concern about long-term planning, and that's when I had to slow them down a bit.

> **One of your main concerns should be the income needs of your surviving spouse.**

My first question when someone asks me about long-term planning is always, "Have you ever considered the income needs of your surviving spouse?" I asked Joe this very question.

Betty and Joe just stared at me. I get it; no one wants to think about the time when their spouse may die. It's a heavy topic and one many people like to avoid. I could tell this couple hadn't talked much about it with each other, so I began prodding them a little further.

I asked them about their work history, and Joe told me he worked for Armstrong for over forty years before retiring. Meanwhile, Betty spent most of her working years as a stay-at-home mother to their two children. I asked about any pensions they were receiving; Joe told me he was getting $4,000 a month from his Armstrong pension, Betty didn't have a pension, and her Social Security was $1,000 a month—less than half of what his was.

In total, Betty and Joe were bringing in $7,000 a month in fixed income payments. Betty proudly said how great it was, adding, "We finally have an income that allows us to do everything we want!" Next, I asked Joe if he took his full pension benefit at retirement. His expression fell, and he confirmed that he had. Betty didn't understand just yet why her husband looked so glum.

"Ma'am, do you know what that means for you?"

Statistically speaking, women outlive men by an average of seven years. Because Joe took his full pension benefit, he elected a payment plan based ONLY on his life expectancy. At his death, the pension payments would stop, and his wife would receive no more payments.

When I explained this to her, I could see Betty's heart sink. At Joe's death, she would be losing over half their income. And it doesn't just stop there. Social Security does not pay both your benefit and your deceased spouse's benefit; it will only pay the higher of the two. And in their case, her husband's Social Security was $2,000 a month.

If—and more likely *when*—Joe predeceases her, she will be taking a 70 percent decrease in her yearly income. That's a HUGE difference. It's also an avoidable mistake.

I don't blame Betty and Joe for this mistake. I blame a lack of education and access to information about spousal poverty and the income gap. Had they been working with a knowledgeable advisor at the time Joe retired, they would not be in this situation. It's heartbreaking. But it wasn't the end of the road for them.

This news was so devastating to Betty that she called me a week later and said they were delaying going to Florida and wanted to see me immediately. I saw them in my office the next day, and we got to work figuring out how to save her from going broke should Joe pass away first. There was a lot to unpack with this couple moving forward.

Since Betty was a stay-at-home mom most of her life, the retirement accounts in her name were small. Joe carried the bulk of their retirement assets, spread across variable annuities and aggressive mutual funds. While it was too late to alter his pension choices, it certainly was not too late to save their investments.

I've mentioned variable annuities before now, but I have yet to delve into exactly what one is. Well, it's just as it sounds. It's an annuity product in which your account balance can vary—and not in a good way.

Many experts agree that variable annuities are the worst retirement investment out there. Personally, I think they should be illegal to sell to anyone.

5 Reasons Why You Should Never Buy A Variable Annuity

Jeff Rose

11-13 minutes

Breathe in.

Smell that?

It's the stench of a variable annuity. If you just threw up a little bit in your mouth, I don't blame you. If you didn't, you probably don't know enough about variable annuities.

Source: https://www.forbes.com/sites/jrose/2015/03/28/5-reasons-why-you-should-never-buy-a-variable-annuity/?sh=2d1776e94c6b

Variable annuities have the most fees out of any investment product out there. And again, none of these fees are being disclosed! Betty and Joe each had an IRA invested in a variable annuity with Jackson National Life Insurance. The account they had was charging them over 7 percent in annual fees.

Variable Annuity Fees

Curious on what types of fees you can expect to pay? Here's a breakdown on what could potentially be eating away at your returns (quotes via the SEC):

- **Mortality and expense risk charge:** "This charge is equal to a certain percentage of your account value, typically in the range of 1.25% per year. This charge compensates the insurance company for insurance risks it assumes under the annuity contract. Profit from the mortality and expense risk charge is sometimes used to pay the insurer's costs of selling the variable annuity, such as a commission paid to your financial professional for selling the variable annuity to you."

- **Administrative fees:** "The insurer may deduct charges to cover record-keeping and other administrative expenses. This may be charged as a flat account maintenance fee (perhaps $25 or $30 per year) or as a percentage of your account value (typically in the range of 0.15% per year)."

- **Underlying fund expenses (sub-accounts):** "You will also indirectly pay the fees and expenses imposed by the mutual funds that are the underlying investment options for your variable annuity."

- **Additional riders:** "Special features offered by some variable annuities, such as a stepped-up death benefit, a guaranteed minimum income benefit, or long-term care insurance, often carry additional fees and charges."

- **Surrender charges:** "If you withdraw money from a variable annuity within a certain period after a purchase payment (typically within six to eight years, but sometimes as long as ten years), the insurance company usually will assess a "surrender" charge, which is a type of sales charge. This charge is used to pay your financial professional a commission for selling the variable annuity to you. Generally, the surrender charge is a percentage of the amount withdrawn, and declines gradually over a period of several years, known as the "surrender period.""

Source: https://www.forbes.com/sites/jrose/2015/03/28/5-reasons-why-you-should-never-buy-a-variable-annuity/

On top of all the fees they were paying, their accounts had only grown 14 percent in the last fifteen years. Remember in chapter 4, I told you how our clients made over 100 percent in their indexed annuities from 2008 to 2018? Well, Betty and Joe had purchased these variable annuities in 2006, which means they were in the market during the same period our clients who were invested in the indexed annuity. Betty and Joe's accounts didn't even make half what our clients made. Had they chosen almost any investment option other than these variable annuities, they would have had over a million dollars in their IRAs by now.

This is why I believe variable annuities should be illegal for any pre-retiree or retiree. The outrageous fees are bad enough, but combined with the risky investment options, I would never recommend a variable annuity to anyone. In fact, every time I see someone come into my office who owns a variable annuity, I recommend they get out of it immediately. I have yet to see one that is worth it.

In the end, I worked with Betty and Joe to create an investment portfolio that would support them now and well beyond Joe's life. Had they gone to Florida without seeing me, they would still have been in those variable annuities when the stock market began its decline in January 2022. Every time I see them, they thank me for our conversation after my workshop that led to them delaying their trip to Florida so they could meet with me. And cases like this are why I truly want to help you and everyone else I can.

CHAPTER 7
KNOW WHEN TO
TAKE SOCIAL SECURITY

If you have not taken your Social Security yet, or you have only started your benefits in the last twelve months, I strongly urge you to come to see me immediately. Much like Joe's pension, Social Security benefits require careful planning and understanding to maximize the benefits during your and your spouse's lifetime. With all that we hear about Social Security, I'm surprised that there isn't more access to income planning regarding Social Security. This is why I offer this service to all my clients, free of charge.

The first step to understanding your Social Security benefits is knowing your *full retirement age (FRA)*. At your FRA, you are entitled to your full Social Security benefits.

BIRTH YEAR	FULL RETIREMENT AGE
1943-1954	66
1955	66 + 2 months
1956	66 + 4 months
1957	66 + 6 months
1958	2.66 + 8 months%
1959	66 + 10 months
1960 and later	67

Source: https://www.socialsecurityintelligence.com/social-security-age-of-retirement/

Once you decide when to apply for Social Security benefits, you'll want to apply no more than four months before the date you wish for your benefits to start. If you've already begun collecting Social Security, and it's been less than twelve months since your first payment, I urge you to come to see me and confirm you started collecting at a time that makes the most sense for you long-term. You must do this within the twelve-month window because this is the only time Social Security allows you to withdraw your application and reapply at a future date. Do keep in mind if you do withdraw your initial application, you will be required to repay any benefits paid up until that point.

Social Security gives you three main choices on when to collect your benefits: before FRA, at FRA, or after FRA.

1 **Start collecting early** Prior to Full Retirement Age	2 **Start collecting at** Full Retirement Age	3 **Start collecting after** Full Retirement Age
Start between age 62 and Full Retirement Age and receive benefits reduced by up to 30%, depending on your year of birth and Full Retirement Age.	Receive 100% of your benefit (Primary Insurance Amount)	Wait and receive benefits that are increased 8% annually up to 32% (depending upon Full Retirement Age) through delayed retirement credits. Credits are available each year past Full Retirement Age that you wait to start collecting until age 70; credits are pro-rated for partial years
PROS		
Potentially collect income over a longer period of time, depending on longevity	Receive the full Social Security benefit earned	Receive a higher benefit amount than otherwise available at Full Retirement Age
CONS		
Reduced monthly benefit for life	Could receive a larger monthly benefit by waiting	Could receive benefits for a shorter period of time, depending on longevity

Source: https://myannuitystore.com/social-security/

If you choose to collect before your FRA, you may do so as early as age sixty-two. However, collecting early comes with some downsides. It could reduce your monthly benefits by up to 30 percent for the rest of your life. If you are still working or decide to go back to work before your FRA, you are limited to how much you can earn per year and still receive your full benefit.

In 2022 when you decide to collect Social Security at age sixty-two, you can only earn a maximum of $19,560 per year; for every two dollars you earn over that limit, your benefits will be reduced by one dollar. Similarly, in the year you reach FRA, you can earn up to $51,960 in the months before you begin collecting your benefit. After reaching your FRA, there is no limit on how much you can earn annually. So, if you are planning to work until 70 but you want to collect Social Security as soon as you reach FRA, you can do both as fully explained on the Social Security Administration (www.ssa.gov/) website.

If you begin your benefits after your FRA, you can increase your benefits by 8 percent annually. You can delay collecting Social Security up until age seventy. Doesn't it sound too good to be true that you can increase your benefits forever? Well, that's because it is . . . sort of.

The question of when to collect is one of the most debated questions when it comes to Social Security benefits, and that's because the answer is different for everyone.

Here's a hypothetical example illustrating how monthly benefit amounts can differ based on the age you choose to collect. In this example, we're assuming your FRA is sixty-six and eight months and that your benefit at FRA is $1,000 per month.

Social Security benefits vary by starting age

Monthly amounts increase for those who delay the age at which they start receiving benefits. The example below assumes a benefit of $1,000 at a full retirement age of 66 and 8 months.

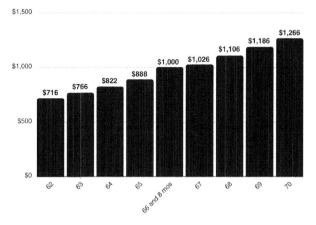

Source: https://www.cnbc.com/2020/01/10/this-costly-social-security-mistake-could-result-in-years-of-regret.html

That extra $266 a month at age seventy looks pretty appealing, doesn't it? Let's look at the table below to help weigh the trade-offs of starting early versus waiting, based on your year of birth and your FRA.

YEAR OF BIRTH	FRA	BENEFIT as a percentage of your Primary Insurance Amount, if you start collecting benefits at age				
		62	63	64	65	66
1943-54	66	75	80	86 2/3	93 1/3	100
1955	66 + 2 months	74 1/6	79 1/6	85 5/9	92 2/9	98 8/9
1956	66 + 4 months	73 1/3	78 1/3	84 4/9	91 1/9	97 7/9
1957	66 + 6 months	72 1/2	77 1/2	83 1/3	90	96 2/3
1958	2.66 + 8 months	71 2/3	76 2/3	82 2/9	88 8/9	95 5/9
1959	66 + 10 months	70 5/6	75 5/6	81 1/9	87 7/9	94 4/9
1960 and later	67	70	75	80	86 2/3	93 1/2

YEAR OF BIRTH	FRA	BENEFIT as a percentage of your Primary Insurance Amount, if you start collecting benefits at age			
		67	68	69	70
1943-54	66	108	116	124	132
1955	66 + 2 months	106 2/3	114 2/3	122 2/3	130 2/3
1956	66 + 4 months	105 1/3	113 1/3	121 1/3	129 1/3
1957	66 + 6 months	104	112	120	128
1958	2.66 + 8 months	102 2/3	110 2/3	118 2/3	126 2/3
1959	66 + 10 months	101 1/3	109 1/3	117 1/3	125 1/3
1960 and later	67	100	108	116	124

Source: From SS savvy booklet

The next item we need to consider is longevity. Longevity plays a key role in determining the best age to begin receiving Social Security benefits. If your family has a history of living long, you could potentially receive more in lifetime benefits by waiting and receiving a higher monthly payment.

The following table shows another hypothetical situation showing total benefits paid through age eighty-five, assuming three common starting ages. In this example, we are assuming that you would receive $1,000 at your FRA of sixty-six.

TOTAL BENEFITS PAID

Age	Start at age 62 Monthly Benefit $725	Start at age 66 and 6 months Monthly Benefit $1,000	Start at age 70 Monthly Benefit $1,280
62	$8,700		
63	17,400		
64	26,100		
65	34,800		
66	43,500	$6,000	
67	52,200	18,000	
68	60,900	30,000	
69	69,600	42,000	
70	78,300	54,000	$15,360
71	87,000	66,000	30,720
72	95,700	78,000	46,080
73	104,400	90,000	61,440
74	113,100	102,000	76,800
75	121,800	114,000	92,160
76	130,500	126,000	107,520
77	139,200	138,000	122,880
78	147,900	150,000	138,240
79	156,600	162,000	153,600
80	165,300	174,000	168,960
81	174,000	186,000	184,320
82	182,700	198,000	199,680
83	191,400	210,000	215,040
84	200,100	222,000	230,400
85	208,800	234,000	245,760

* Starting benefits at age 66 and 6 months will generate more total income beginning at age 78

* Starting benefits at age 70 and 6 months will generate more total income beginning at age 82

Source: From SS savvy booklet

You can see that by collecting early in this example, you will never catch up to your benefits received by waiting until FRA. However, I always tell my clients that if waiting is going to cause a strain on their finances at the time, it always makes sense to collect.

In the last chapter, I mentioned that at Joe's passing, Betty will lose her Social Security benefit but will be able to take his higher benefit. This is true for you too. When your spouse passes away, you are entitled to retain whoever's benefit was higher. In Betty's case, Joe's benefit was twice hers, so she would drop her benefit and take his at his death. If your benefit is higher than your spouse's, then you would keep your benefit, but lose theirs.

You don't necessarily have to be married to collect this spousal benefit. If you were previously married for at least ten years but divorced and have not since remarried, you may be entitled to your ex-spouse's benefits after their death.

I could write an entire book on the complexities of Social Security if I wanted to, but that's not what I'm here to do. I'm here to teach you how to best plan for your retirement as a whole. So, let's get into how retirement planning and Social Security go hand in hand.

As I mentioned in the last chapter, higher taxes reduce the money in your pocket each year. But how exactly does it affect your income? Based on your income level, up to 85 percent of your Social Security benefits may be subjected to income taxes.

By allocating a portion of your retirement assets to the tax-deferred indexed annuity, you may be able to significantly decrease your taxable income, potentially allowing you to keep more of your Social Security benefits.

Under current tax law, annuity growth does not count towards your income as long as you keep that money in the account. When you do decide to take a withdrawal from your annuity, only then are the annuity earnings taxed and the income included in calculating the tax due on your Social Security earnings.

SECTION 3:
YOUR LONG-TERM PLAN

"It's not how old you are. It's how prepared you are."

Whatever your age, I have taken some steps in the previous two sections to help you do the "pre-work" or homework needed to understand your financial picture.

Taking action on this new knowledge will go a long way to creating a comfortable future financial life for yourself, whether you are already retired, still working, experiencing a major life change, or in the earliest stages of thinking about retirement.

I have shared with you some words about risk. I have told some cautionary stories to show how difficult it can be to choose the right advisor to help secure your financial future and revealed the red flags you must look for in your relationship with advisors and your financial structuring. Yes, the investment industry is complex; there are so many options out there that are confusing.

Some might say that the financial industry is loaded like a blackjack table in Las Vegas, where the house (or your traditional advisor) always wins. You now have new information and a new awareness about your advisor and advisor fees, what can happen to your hard-earned money, and what a great advisor should do for you.

I want you to know that there is no need to do it alone when you are trying to understand and plan for your elder-year needs, so the right advisor is a big key to success. I have also briefly discussed taxes and Social Security—which, let's face it, are daunting topics for us all!

> **I'm here to clarify things for you.
> We are in this together!**

Hopefully, even at this point in your reading, you feel better armed. Perhaps your new education and knowledge have shown you some of the changes you'll need to make. Good. Be prepared now to make *some more* changes to your investments, whether small or more dramatic, and to your way of thinking about your money.

Why more? What else can there be?

As my family learned from caring for Helen, financial planning is not all about how much money you have and where it is invested. Planning should include a serious look at your health needs in your elder years. It should also account for your retirement wish list of activities and goals, including how to pay for them.

All this is to say you need to include more than "portfolio discussions" in your retirement planning. When you tie it all together with the next information I'll be sharing, you will be doing all you can to take care of yourself in your later years.

In this next section, it is time to move into actual planning. To do this, you should talk to an independent fiduciary like The Richardson Group. Doing so will help you consider not just the financial side of your life, but also the legal aspects, the healthcare aspects, and the legacy you choose to leave after your death.

I'll walk you through each type of planning, starting with the legal aspects of your plan, then long-term care, and discuss the possibilities you have for income for life. Because we can't predict our future or the future of your health, you need to know that you can change any part of your financial organization to ensure your elder years will be effortless and seamless—and financially secure.

CHAPTER 8
DON'T BE AFRAID OF LONG-TERM CARE

A conversation no one likes having is discussing what happens when or if you need skilled care. Much like talking about death, talking about nursing homes is just as uncomfortable. Typically, men do not live as long as women and therefore end up needing nursing care before their female counterparts. For many of you reading this book, you may very well have to deal with the possibility of your husband going to a nursing home before you.

Don't be like Joe and Betty and avoid the difficult conversations of long-term planning; it's imperative you know all the facts and have a plan in place in case you or a loved one goes to a nursing home.

Typically, when I ask my clients if they have considered what happens if one or both of them end up in a nursing home, they tend to give me a *"yeah... we've thought about it... sort of..."* To be fair, when I'm asking my clients this, they are healthy, in good shape, and feeling fine. Nursing homes aren't on their minds. Even if you can imagine the fact that you may end up in a nursing home, you most likely are not going to admit that when you're talking to me, or anyone else. It can feel embarrassing to talk about, but it's nothing you should be ashamed of.

Let's imagine you've planned a trip abroad with your girlfriends, your spouse, or your sister. Whenever you plan a trip, you always hope for the best, but you often may plan for the worst. You might buy travel insurance in case of an emergency, or maybe you insure your plane tickets in case plans change. You never know what could happen during your vacation—or your life.

Whenever you ride an airplane, there's always the possibility something *could* happen, even though it's unlikely. Now, let's say you're going on a trip, pick any place you'd like. Let's imagine we're going to Rome, Italy.

You've packed your bags, left early enough for the airport in case of traffic, and now you're checking your bags and getting your tickets. Italy has never felt closer. But you're not there yet! You still have to deal with the hassle of TSA. You remove your shoes, belt, and jacket, put your laptop in a separate bin, and take out all your toiletries. And then once everything has been checked by security, you hustle to get it all packed away again.

You maneuver your way through a sea of people to find your gate just to sit and wait some more. Finally, your section is called, and you gather yourself to stand in another line as you shuffle onto the plane. There's hardly any storage space left; your bag has to be put five rows in front of you, but at least you're finally settled. Italy is only a few hours away now.

As the crew prepares for takeoff, the pilot welcomes everyone aboard the aircraft. He explains you'll be flying miles above the ground going hundreds of miles an hour, and some turbulence may be expected along the way, but not to worry.

Everything seems standard; the pilot's right. *"Don't worry,"* says the pilot. But then, the pilot adds, "Oh yeah . . . one more thing. We have about a 50 percent chance of making it to Italy today safely. So, folks, have a great flight!"

The moment everyone hears that they're all running for the exits! Who would stay on that flight? No one would stay on a plane with a 50-50 chance of arriving safely. Even going on your dream vacation is not worth that risk.

Well, what if I told you that those were the same odds of you or your spouse needing end-of-life care?

With those odds, at least one of you is going to need assistance at some point, if not both of you. So now that we know this is a real possibility, what can you do?

When I ask my clients this after explaining the likelihood of needing long-term care, they tell me they will use their savings, money they never intended to spend, which is a great plan—maybe. Before I get into that, let's discuss the type of care you may need.

Very rarely does one go straight from healthy living to needing skilled nursing care. Usually, going to a nursing home is a gradual process that can take years—and lots of money. The three stages of care are:

1. In-home care

2. Assisted living

3. Skilled nursing care

Not everyone needs to go through all three stages, but most people do experience a gradual decline in health.

With in-home care, a nurse will come to the home to check in throughout the day. Typically, in-home care is the first step, especially if one spouse is still living at the home but cannot necessarily care for their ailing spouse. In-home care becomes necessary when you or your spouse can longer perform two of the six daily activities of living:

- Feeding oneself

- Bathing oneself

- Dressing oneself

- Toileting oneself (including getting on and off alone)

- Transferring oneself (getting in and out of bed, getting from one room to another)

- Maintaining continence

Essentially, if you find that you can no longer cook for yourself or can't get around easily, it may be time to consider in-home care. Again, this is nothing to be ashamed of. In fact, I urge anyone who needs home care to get it if you can, because having extra help may prevent further injury in the future.

The next step is assisted living, which becomes necessary when you need more regular care. Maybe you are experiencing memory issues and need someone to ensure you are taking the correct medications at the right time. Maybe you no longer just have trouble cooking, but also have trouble lifting the food to your mouth or even trouble swallowing. Essentially, you are not so immobile that you need skilled care, but your health has degraded enough that you need more regular care and the availability to ring someone for help.

When you're in assisted living, you're usually living in an apartment owned by a nursing home, and there's always someone on call to help you. You're no longer in your home at this point, but typically these apartments can be made to feel like home. You don't have a roommate or hospital equipment around you, but there's often an emergency button you can push. Many often have cafeterias and community centers. With assisted living, you are still very much on your own, but there's extra help anytime you need it.

Many of you may eventually end up in a skilled nursing care facility: a nursing home. If you have severe dementia or Alzheimer's, you may need to be watched 24/7; this is when a nursing home is the next move. If your health deteriorates so much you cannot care for yourself, skilled care is necessary.

Once you're in a nursing home, there's really no way to know how long you'll be there. You may be there for a few months, or you could be like my grandmother Helen and be there for years.

Financially, each of these stages of care can be pretty expensive. Home care is an hourly rate, with an average of fifty dollars an hour just for someone to help with a few things. If you need someone to come to your home for just ten hours a week, that could cost you a minimum of $2,000 a month. Assisted living is double that! Typically, assisted living facilities cost between $3,500 to $5,000 a month. And if you think that's expensive, nursing homes average around $10,000 a month. And keep in mind that Medicaid will only help with nursing home care expenses, not in-home or assisted care.

I know, you are probably not feeling any better about facing a nursing home, but it's important to know what you may be looking at in terms of long-term care. Keep in mind, over 50 percent of people will go to a nursing home. Those odds are not exactly in your favor, which is why you really need to financially prepare yourself.

If I told you there was a 50 percent chance your bank would close next year, you'd withdraw all your money and take it elsewhere, wouldn't you? If the pilot tells you there's only a 50 percent chance you'll make it to your destination, you're getting off that plane, aren't you? Well, end-of-life care is your 50 percent. What can you do to protect yourself?

Even in a nursing home, there are still ways to protect your money. I'm about to bust every myth you've probably ever heard about nursing homes.

Being able to protect your money, even after being admitted to a nursing home, is the one thing my parents wish they had known when my grandmother needed nursing care. As I explained, they took care of Helen for eight years in their home, and then she spent another eight years in a nursing home. When Helen lived with my family, my parents took on all the burden themselves. Their lives were completely transformed to help Helen and never had any financial help in doing so.

Helen's memory declined quickly, and along with it, her physical health. It felt as though she went from being strong and independent to completely dependent overnight. She was a prime example of someone you'd never expect to need such advanced care, yet she was one of the 50 percent.

Because of how hard it was to care for Helen, my parents sought out how to help others, and now it's a part of everything we still do for our clients. The strategies I'm about to outline will help you tremendously in dealing with end-of-life care for yourself, your spouse, and your loved ones.

First, during those years of in-home care, Helen was eligible for a benefit known as "Aid and Attendance."[3] If you or your spouse are a veteran, served at least twenty-four hours (yes, hours), and were on reserve for ninety days thereafter, during an active time of war, you may be eligible for these benefits. Aid and Attendance offers up to $2,600 a month to use towards in-home care, assisted living, and even nursing home care.

However, like most government benefits, it is not easy to acquire. I encourage everyone to apply, but

---

3   "The Aid & Attendance Benefit," American Veterans Aid, https://americanveteransaid. com/aid-attendance-benefit.

for most people, their application is rejected for being "over-resourced." That means, according to the VA, you have too many assets. In other words, you have too much money!

So, what can you do? If you work with me, I can show you. Even if you have too much money today, we can rearrange your assets and utilize a different kind of annuity to help you qualify.

You're more than welcome to go to the VA on your own and apply, but again if you're over-resourced, you'll be denied, and the representatives working there won't be able to help you. Sure, applying on your own will save you some money, but working with me will help you save *most* of your money and obtain the benefit you're entitled to.

Now if you were paying attention, you know the Aid and Attendance benefit is not enough to cover nursing home costs, and that's if you even qualify for it. I'm sure everyone has heard that nursing homes will take all your money before you're gone, but I'm going to tell you how that does not need to be true for you.

Once you find yourself or your spouse needing nursing care, you're going to hear people telling you to *spend down.* Basically, they're going to tell you to spend away your assets to a predetermined amount. Generally, the Spend Down limit, if you're married, is $120,000 and as low as $8,500, if you're single. Say goodbye to all that money you worked so hard to protect—the nursing home wants it all.

Don't panic yet! I know you're concerned, and if you didn't have this book, you should be! Most people don't believe they can protect themselves; they just hope they aren't in the 50 percent of people needing skilled care.

Thankfully, you have me, and you don't need to worry. For married couples, I can help you protect 100 percent of your assets, and for individuals, I can help you protect 50 percent of your assets from nursing home Spend Down.

Many people will tell you one way to save your money from the nursing home is just to spend it! Put a new roof on your house, buy a new car, redo your kitchen. But what good does that do? All your money is gone then, anyway. Instead, I can help you save almost all your money without having to throw it all away.

I worked with a couple a few years ago and helped them save over $1,000,000. The husband had accumulated $1.5 million in savings for them to use in retirement and eventually pass on to their children. When it came time for him to go to a nursing home, the home was thrilled to have him since he had such a sizeable estate. They assumed the $1.5 million would be theirs.

Too bad for the nursing home, though, because this couple was a client of ours.

Within a month, we had all of his assets rearranged to be in his wife's name, and the nursing home couldn't touch it. You see, as long as one spouse is still at home, the nursing home cannot take the house or spouse's assets, only the assets of the person needing care. But in this couple's case, all the assets were owned by the husband because he was working when his wife was at home taking care of the kids.

What we did is transfer his assets into a *Medicaid-compliant annuity*, a special annuity that allows you to qualify for Medicaid. When the husband's assets were transferred to this annuity, he was essentially broke; all the wealth was transferred to his wife. Now he was completely eligible for Medicaid assistance, while still living in the nursing home of his choice. To this day, his wife is still alive and has all the money they saved.

For those of you who have been widowed, divorced, or never married, you can also save your assets. In cases like this, I would do what we call "half-loaf planning." You see, the married couple gets the whole loaf, and the individual gets half a loaf. Essentially, we can still save 50 percent of your assets from the nursing home, and all the money can still go to your family after you're gone.

Another myth many people hear is that a nursing home can also take your house. When you work with me, one important lesson I'll teach you is this: That is simply not true! There are several reasons why you want to keep your house—one of those is so your beneficiaries can sell it and keep the money after you're gone.

In many cases, the nursing home will ask you to sell your home and give them the proceeds, especially if your monetary assets alone do not qualify you for their facility. This is never true if one spouse is still living in the home. But, if your spouse has already gone into a nursing home or has passed, your home is up for grabs.

I often have clients ask me if they should gift their home to their child to save it from a nursing home. I *strongly* urge you not to do this! I once had a client gift their home to their son, who was able to legally evict his elderly parents! It was so sad to see that happen. Your kids may not be that evil, but gifting your home could still fall into Medicaid's five-year lookback, thus disqualifying you from assistance.

So how do you protect your home?

You use an *"Intent to Return Home Letter."* With this letter, you state your *intent* to return home before passing, thus the home cannot be used as a countable asset. Sounds simple enough, right? Well, that's because it is!

We can agree that, for most people, going to a nursing home is the end of the road. But even still, it should be everyone's intention to return to their home.

INTENT TO RETURN HOME STATEMENT

INSTRUCTIONS: This form is to be completed and signed by the patient or the patient's legal guardian or authorized representative and filed in the case record as documentation.

_____ owns homestead property located at
(Name of Patient)

_____ , _____ ,
(Street)   (City)

_____ , _____ .
(County)   (State)

Although the aforenamed individual is not currently residing in the above designated homestead property, he/she or his/her authorized representative has been interviewed and he/she has stated that it is his/her or the patient's intent to:

Check one of return home these boxes

☐ return home

☐ not return home

_____
(Date)

_____
(Signature of Patient or Authorized Representative)

_____
(Date)

_____
(Signature of Medicaid Eligibility Worker)

The South Carolina Department of Health and Human Services (SCDHHS) complies with applicable Federal civil rights laws and does not discriminate on the basis of race, color, national origin, age, disability, or sex. SCDHHS provides free aids and services to people with disabilities, such as qualified sign language interpreters and written information in other formats (including large print, braille, audio, accessible electronic formats, and other formats). We provide free language services to people whose primary language is not English, such as qualified interpreters and information written in other languages.

DHHS Form 1277 ME (April 2009)

Source: http://www1.scdhhs.gov/internet/eligfm/FM%201277%20ME.pdf

I worked with another couple, John and Jennifer, who had been together for decades before John's Parkinson's advanced so much that he needed skilled care. For Jennifer, it was a double blow. Not only was her husband leaving for a nursing home, but she was also worried she would lose everything in the process.

John and Jennifer had accumulated around $300,000 in savings, plus a house worth $150,000, a car, and their possessions. When John went to the nursing home, she was worried she'd lose it all. She was calling her children trying to figure out which one she would go live with. When she came to see me and expressed these concerns, I calmed her down and told her that even in the worst-case scenario, the nursing home would only spend her down to $120,000, and she would still have the house, the car, and her possessions. That relieved her quite a bit, and she was ready to accept that fate as good enough.

But I don't like my clients to just settle for good enough. That sounds a lot like "suitable." If you recall, I do what's in your best interest, not just what's good enough or suitable for you.

I told Jennifer during our meeting that I could help her protect everything, not just the $120,000. That really piqued her interest. I explained exactly how I could help her save the entire $300,000 by transferring John's assets into her name via the Medicaid-compliant annuity. I did this for her even though her husband was already in the nursing home. And once that money was transferred, I know John felt more at peace leaving his wife in their home, and Jennifer certainly did, too.

Baby boomer women are more likely to experience spousal poverty. Baby boomer men were more likely to work during the years their wives were at home raising their children, thus causing more women to hold fewer assets than their husbands. Men are also more likely to enter a nursing home than women. Without my help, the nursing home is allowed to eat up a husband's IRA, leaving his wife with nothing other than $120,000 in savings, a house, and a car.[4]

Unsurprisingly, nursing homes know the same secrets I'm telling you. However, it's not in their best interest to tell you these things. There's no incentive for them to tell you this. Their strategy is to spend you down to as little as possible before Medicaid kicks in. When Medicaid starts, the nursing home makes about 40 percent less than they do when you pay them directly.

What we do for you is make you eligible for Medicaid in advance—right after you get admitted, in fact. Nursing homes won't have time to spend you down because we'll work quickly to transfer your assets out of their grasp.

---

4   "Boomers don't have nearly enough retirement savings, especially women," Jason
     Lalljee and Hillary Hoffower, January 19, 2022, Insider, https://www.businessinsider.
     com/boomers-dont-have-retirement-savings-women-have-less-than-men-2022-1.

This secret is so well kept that we even had a woman from the Medicaid office working for us at one point who didn't even know this was possible. She's not the only "expert" in this field who doesn't know this. Most professionals don't.

The woman who worked for us had previously worked for the state of Pennsylvania for sixteen years, and her job was to make sure the government got every last penny before any aid kicked in. After working there and before working with us, she also worked for an elder law attorney in the county for nine years. You'd think she would have known about this option, having worked in the industry for so long. Heck, she even told us that what we were doing wasn't allowed.

The elder law firm she worked for just told their clients to spend down their assets before going to the nursing home, but not how to protect the assets. This may seem like a moot point, but it is important to avoid doing everything through one person. Although that elder law attorney didn't understand how to protect people's assets, I suppose we shouldn't expect him to know financial processes, the same way I shouldn't be expected to know most legal processes. But do keep in mind that when it comes to long-term care planning, working with a knowledgeable lawyer is necessary. They don't have to help you with these strategies on their own—that's what I'm for—but you want to make sure you are getting good advice.

Same goes when dealing with advisors. At this point in your life, it's imperative that you work with someone who has a thorough knowledge of long-term care planning. Understanding Medicaid, how to apply for it, and how to get Medicaid is a skill you should always look for in an advisor. This is especially crucial because if you don't have smart advisors who know what they're doing, you're open to potential risk. There are plenty of cases where transfers were not done correctly, and the government came after people's families to recoup the money. Some states even allow Medicaid to go after children to repay for their parents' mistakes.

I know you don't want this to be you. This is a nightmare scenario, but I hope this new information you now have puts your mind at ease.

As you can see, there are plenty of reasons to work with advisors like The Richardson Group who know exactly how to safely shift your money into the right accounts to best benefit you and your family.

CHAPTER 9
ESTATE PLANNING

One thing I really stress to my clients is the importance of getting their affairs in order for their families. This might seem like a no-brainer, but you'd be surprised how many people don't know where their parents or loved ones keep their assets. Many of my clients are interested in leaving a legacy of some kind for their families, but they can't do that without proper planning.

While we're not lawyers, we tell all our clients they should file certain key legal documents, all expertly prepared by an estate planning attorney. You may have an attorney who specializes in estate planning; if not, ask us for a recommendation. I'll address estate planning briefly now.

Estate planning typically starts with drafting and signing a *power of attorney (POA)*. It continues with a *will*. The power of attorney document names an individual who can act on your behalf when you are no longer able. Typically, your POA kicks in when your mental health starts declining, but I've also seen people use their POA when they can no longer physically sign for themselves. You want to be very selective in who you choose as your POA because they will be able to conduct financial transactions such as writing checks, opening new brokerage accounts, closing bank accounts, paying bills, opening new credit cards, etc. A POA is in charge of anything financially related.

> **It's best to get a power of attorney drafted by a lawyer.**

You'll need original documentation to get the POA on file with your accounts. Do keep in mind, however, that banks often require their own POA paperwork. If you are someone's POA, never sign anything such as a POA authorization until the company has accepted the documentation. Otherwise, your signature is useless, and you'll need to do the paperwork all over again.

Why hand over specific authority to someone else? Life can turn on a dime. You never know if you'll get in an accident and become seriously incapacitated. If you were to develop a long-term illness preventing you from taking care of your own business, you'd want to designate someone else to do so. Most of my clients have a POA on file before they're completely reliant on that person.

In the case of married couples, typically you would act as each other's power of attorney, so long as you are still of sound mind and body. You want to make sure you trust the individual you give power of attorney to and be sure that they can handle everything you list. Who to choose might mean having serious discussions within your family or closest circle of friends. You also need to ascertain if the chosen individual agrees. I find that bringing up the topic and talking about it with people you love or respect gives you new insights on who to choose for this role.

The next document you need to have is your will. Most people I meet with either don't have a will, or it's so outdated that it's useless. In Pennsylvania, if you don't have a will, all of your assets go through *probate*—the process where a judge oversees the division of your assets. Probate can be lengthy and expensive. After a certain amount of time, if no one comes forward to claim your assets, it becomes property of the state. Save your loved ones the trouble and have an up-to-date will!

You'll also want to name at least one person to be your *executor*. Your POA can also be your executor, but you need to outline this in your will because the POA position dies with you. At death, your power of attorney can no longer act on your behalf, and now the executor oversees managing affairs.

Even if you believe you don't have enough assets to bother with a will, I suggest you still have one. If you have promised the house to your son after you die, but your brother wants to get his hands on it, your brother could go to court to try and "prove" the house is meant for him. By having a will, you eliminate any uncertainty of who gets what. Note that your life insurance and annuities do not go through probate or a will; the proceeds will go directly to whoever is named a beneficiary on your policies.

Also, make sure the person or people you name in your will as executor(s) knows where the printed will is located. Only you and your attorney really need to see and know what is in your will before you die, but that doesn't mean that the existence of your will needs to be a secret from the people who will take care of things when you're gone.

You might think you'll know where all your money is being kept or where you've stored the last few years of tax returns when the time comes to need these items, but the truth is you never know when that day will come. I know facing your own mortality is a scary thing to do, but it's an important one. My friend and his family recently experienced this firsthand when Jacob, my friend's grandfather, passed away.

Jacob was married to his wife, Jane, for decades and handled everything for the two of them. At his funeral, the pastor even mentioned how much of an attentive husband Jacob was, always caring for his wife.

Even at age ninety, Jacob had been in perfect health, whereas his wife's health was declining; at the time, he was planning a future that more than likely saw Jane predeceasing him. But then he had a serious accident, which led to his untimely death. Up until the accident, he was in good health, and Jacob thought he had time to get his affairs in order for his wife. He was the person who controlled the money in their marriage. He managed multiple properties and various investment accounts on his own. While I don't believe Jacob withheld information from his wife to be malicious, it would have benefited her greatly to know these things.

When he passed away, everything fell apart. He did not have a formal living will, so his family didn't have any documentation to support what his wishes would have been in the hospital. A living will outlines, for example, if you wish to be intubated or resuscitated after an accident; without that documentation, the doctors have to try everything to keep you alive, even if you wish to pass without their intervention. Jane didn't know where most of the passwords were, and even if she did, she didn't know every account they had. Luckily, her children were a great help, but even they only knew so much.

Jane's daughter was telling me a story about an envelope they once got in the mail. It contained a statement showing a dividend that was recently paid to the now-deceased Jacob; it was only a few dollars. Being diligent, Jacob's family went to the bank to get the necessary documents to obtain information about this account, and upon doing so, they learned the account had almost $500,000! Who knows how long it would have taken to find that account if the family had just chucked the statement thinking it wasn't worth much?

Jacob's unpreparedness should motivate you to get your affairs in order now while you still can. Each time I work with a new client, I gift them an estate planning binder with a tab for each document they should have. The spine of the binder also says "Estate Planning" so their family can easily locate it on their shelf. I also tell my clients, at the very least, to list the company names where they have accounts so their family isn't calling around to every brokerage in town. Put the business cards of your lawyer and advisor in a binder like this as well; being prepared really will make all the difference.

I mentioned earlier how careful you should be when choosing a POA or executor, but you should also give beneficiaries careful consideration. Most accounts you own allow you to list beneficiaries, and if they give you the option, I highly recommend you do.

For most assets, you will find that you are able to list both primary and contingent beneficiaries. When you pass, your money will go to your primary beneficiaries, if they are still living. If your primary beneficiaries predecease you, then the money will go to your contingent beneficiaries. If you only list your spouse, and you are both killed in an accident together, it can be very tricky for your loved ones to receive the death benefit proceeds from life insurance or annuities, even if it's outlined in your will as to who gets what. It's good practice to at least list one contingent beneficiary, if possible.

When your relationship with anyone you've named beneficiary changes, it's best to update your beneficiaries as soon as possible. In many states, Pennsylvania being one of them, a named beneficiary is entitled to death proceeds, and contesting their right to it is nearly impossible. If you still have your ex-husband listed as the beneficiary to an old life insurance policy, even if you've remarried and updated your will, beware: If you die without changing the beneficiary names, your new husband is not entitled to that money at all. If you recall, I said earlier that life insurance and annuities circumvent probate. The death proceeds on these policies get paid to whoever is listed as a beneficiary, and the will won't matter.

I often have clients who want to leave money for their grandchildren, which I think is lovely. However, naming minors as beneficiaries of life insurance or annuities can be a little complicated. Minors cannot own legal property in their name until they reach age eighteen. When annuities or life insurance are left to a minor, the child's parent or guardian must become involved to prove guardianship, and the account will not be accessible to the child until they become an adult. Because of this, I urge my clients to leave the money to the child's parents or another trusted adult.

	USING UTMA STATEGY	NOT USING UTMA STRATEGY
Owner/ Annuitant	Grandpa Joe Smith	Grandpa Joe Smith
Beneficiary Designation on Application	Ben Sr. as custodian for Ben Jr. under the California Uniform Transfers to Minors Act (UTMA)	Ben Jr.
At Owner's Death	Claim form completed by custodian, Ben Sr.	Claim form typically requires guardian's documentation obtained through the courts
Result	No additional cost; court intervention not necessary	Additional cost/delay involved in setting up guardianship; court intervention likely

Source: https://www.annuities.pacificlife.com/home/insights/blog/2019/minor-oversights-can-have-big-consequences.html

There are also two common types of beneficiaries: *revocable* and *irrevocable*. Revocable beneficiaries are the most common and provide the most flexibility for the account holder. A revocable beneficiary can be changed by the account owner at any time, allowing for beneficiary updates as life changes. Irrevocable beneficiaries are less common, but often offered as an option with most policies; however, an irrevocable beneficiary can never be changed.

I have a client who exercises her ability to change her revocable beneficiaries a little too often. This client has a pretty large account with us, and she has named her two nephews as primary beneficiaries. She calls us all the time and changes her beneficiaries, based on how nice one or both of her nephews are being to her. If the one hasn't called or visited in a while, she will give his brother a higher percentage of the inheritance! What is funny is they have no idea this auntie of theirs is loaded—the nephews have no idea how much money their aunt has or that they are beneficiaries of any of it! I hope she keeps some kind of record of all these changes to present at the reading of her will.

If there's anything to take away from this chapter, it's that I want you to be prepared. Updating your will or having POA paperwork drawn up should not cost you a lot of money. And if you find the law offices you've called are quoting outrageous prices, call me. I can either help

you find free resources to update your estate documents
or point you in the direction of a knowledgeable and
affordable estate planning attorney.

CHAPTER 10
FUNERAL PLANNING

The latter half of this book is filled with all kinds of cheery topics, huh? I've given myself the task of providing you with the vital information to preserve your wealth and give you and your loved ones peace of mind. So here is another "cheery" topic: funerals.

Most people avoid *funeral planning*. It's one thing to talk about what your spouse should do if you die; it's an entirely different thing going and picking out caskets together.

Just like nursing homes, funeral homes are a big business. Don't let funeral directors fool you; they're just salespeople. And, oftentimes, they use your family's grief to drive up their profits. When you leave the funeral planning to your family after your death, they can talk them into spending more than you would have. What could have been a $10,000 funeral now costs your family $20,000!

I urge all my clients to preplan their funerals. Most funeral homes are happy to preplan with you, especially because they know you're coming back. Preplanning allows you to choose exactly what type of casket, headstone, or urn you'd like; you can plan how much you'd like to spend on floral arrangements or a reception. Again, typically, when you preplan your own funeral, the costs are much less than what your grieving family would spend. It's a lot easier to pick the just-as-nice-but-cheaper pine casket yourself than it is for your family to pass on the much-more-expensive mahogany casket.

Funeral homes will typically allow you to preplan and lock in a final price even without prepaying the funeral home directly. I strongly advise against prepaying a funeral director.

TOP STORIES

Funeral home director pleads guilty to stealing from elderly

October 23, 2019

A Pennsylvania funeral home director who authorities say stole a half million dollars' worth of funeral policy payments from the elderly has pleaded guilty to theft and forgery.

Source: https://www.wpxi.com/news/top-stories/
funeral-home-director-pleads-guilty-to-stealing-from-elderly-1/1000699211/

Unfortunately, this is not the only example of funeral directors stealing from their clients.

One way to avoid both having your money stolen and prepaying your funeral is by using a *Medicaid Exempt Funeral Trust*. A Medicaid Exempt Funeral Trust is an excellent tool to utilize when it comes to paying for your funeral and for nursing home planning! The trust really serves two purposes: prepaying your funeral and protecting the prepayment for the nursing home.

Pennsylvania allows an individual to purchase a funeral trust for up to $18,500 or a combined $37,000 per couple. When applying for the trust, it's very simple. There is no underwriting, such as is typical with final expense life insurance policies, also known as burial insurance. You can either designate the funeral home of your choice at the time of application, you can leave it blank until later, or even wait until after death. In fact, many people purchase a funeral trust and never list a funeral home because they only ever intended for the proceeds to be paid to their beneficiaries. This is what makes it a great tool for nursing home planning, as well.

When you do pass away, the trust pays for your funeral expenses, and any remaining cash balance is directed to your estate to be divided amongst your beneficiaries. There are no fees to set up or maintain a funeral trust, and it even earns nominal interest during the lifetime of the policy. Many policies also allow for flexible payment options, such as an upfront lump sum or a monthly payment plan for a term of your choosing.

One thing to keep in mind, however, is that a Medicaid Exempt Funeral Trust is irrevocable. Once you purchase this type of plan, the money is only accessible at death, no exceptions. The second reason you should have a funeral trust is the money is 100 percent Medicaid exempt. Just like the Medicaid-compliant annuity I talked about in the previous chapter, a funeral trust also can help you qualify for Medicaid.

Funeral trusts are also a better option compared to burial insurance because insurance policies are not Medicaid exempt, and a nursing home can use the cash value from life insurance to pay for your bills. Nursing homes cannot access the money in a funeral trust and having a funeral trust will not disqualify you from admittance either. The last thing a nursing home wants to do is spend down all your money and then have to pay for your funeral. Funeral trusts are widely welcomed at nursing homes.

The Medicaid-compliant annuities are very complicated to set up and are best utilized in cases where a couple has jointly owned assets above the $120,000 Spend Down limit or in cases where an individual has assets over $80,000. Although the Spend Down limit for individuals is much lower than $80,000, singles fall under the "half-loaf" plan, where they can save 50 percent of the assets. Because of the complexity of the Medicaid-compliant annuity, the more assets you have, the better suited you are for the annuity.

If your assets are below those amounts, this is when funeral trust planning really comes into play. With a married couple, the nursing home cannot leave the at-home spouse with less than $120,000, so a funeral trust is not necessary at that time. We would utilize a funeral trust when one spouse passes and now the second spouse is headed to a nursing home.

If the wife, for example, is the surviving spouse going to a nursing home, she can be spent down to as little as $8,500 before qualifying for Medicaid. If we used the annuity, that would save about $60,000. It still doesn't qualify her for Medicaid, and the other $60,000 would be spent down to nothing before Medicaid kicked in.

In this case, we could also utilize the funeral trust and set aside an additional $18,500. With a total of about $88,000 saved, she will qualify for Medicaid more quickly, and her beneficiaries will stand to inherit a little more.

As I'm writing this book, in fact, I'm helping a client utilize a funeral trust so she can qualify for Medicaid. The unfortunate part about nursing homes is that without any assets, you'll end up at a state-run Medicaid facility. With ample assets, you get to choose where you go, but for most people, the entire cost is out-of-pocket. If you fall into the category of not-enough-assets-to-pay-for-private-care, but still have too-much-money-to-qualify-for-Medicaid, you're out of luck. With too few assets, a private nursing home won't accept you, but a Medicaid facility won't take you if you have too much.

Another client I'm helping now falls into the category of having "too much" to qualify for Medicaid. Currently, he has about $27,000 in assets and is trying to qualify for Medicaid so he can receive skilled care. What I'm doing for him is cashing out his annuity policy, worth about $20,000, and withholding 10 percent for taxes on that amount, so he will net right around $18,000 cash from the policy. We will then take the proceeds from the annuity and a little extra from savings and buy a funeral trust for $18,500. This will then drop his asset limit to $8,500, thus qualifying him for Medicaid. When he eventually passes, the money from the trust can be used to cover any burial expenses and provide a small inheritance for his son.

Funeral trusts are also easily accessible. Of course, I offer these to my clients. Many banks also offer funeral trusts. I've even seen funeral homes offering funeral trusts in exchange for locking in a preplanned price. Whatever option best suits your needs, I suggest you use it. However, I always recommend buying a policy through me or another trusted representative so you can be confident you're getting the best advice.

CHAPTER 11
INCOME FOR LIFE

Income for as long as you live after retirement from the world of work and earning might seem not only like a pipe dream to many people but can be a significant worry. None of our clients want to be a burden on their loved ones in their later years.

I see clients with $30,000 who are concerned that it's not going to last their whole lifetime. Likewise, I see people with $800,000 who are more than worried that this amount is not going to last for the rest of their lives. Everyone shares this same concern.

None of us want to sit on the sofa with the remote in our hands all day long during retirement. We have bucket lists, wish lists, and goals! We have places to go and people to see! While not all the items on these lists cost money, we'll first help you figure out which ones do. It is important to know how much money you will need during retirement—at least as close as you can get to a true number.

I've said it before, and I'll say it again: The bulk of your money at retirement should *not* be in the stock market! High fees and high risk are the biggest threats to the longevity of your retirement fund.

Stay away from aggressive and costly mutual funds, avoid volatile stocks, and steer clear of government bonds as interest rates rise. I also urge you to stay away from variable annuities and any annuity offering a bonus or income rider.

Variable annuities are hands-down the worst annuity and investment product out there. The fees are often upwards of 5 percent, and they are incredibly risky! I do *not* recommend a variable annuity to *anyone*.

I met a couple this summer with a variable annuity older than me. Two decades ago, the client told his advisor he wanted to be in a fixed annuity, so the advisor told him he would keep him in the variable annuity but move his money into a fixed option earning 3 percent. If you like guaranteed interest, 3 percent is not a terrible deal. However, the advisor failed to mention that the minimum fee he could collect on the policy was 2 percent, meaning this client was only getting 1 percent on his money for almost 25 years. This advisor could have easily switched this client into a 3 percent fixed annuity with no fees, but he didn't. He made more money off this client from the variable annuity's fee structure than the client made.

Annuities with *income riders* are other products I steer my clients away from. Almost any annuity out there offers the possibility to add an income rider to your policy. What exactly does this mean?

An income rider is an addition to your annuity policy you can elect at the time of purchase. In its simplest form, if you elect the income rider, it gives you the option to activate the rider and receive fixed monthly payments for a guaranteed period, typically your lifetime. While this sounds like a great deal, there's more to it. For some people, depending on very specific circumstances, a fixed income is exactly what they need. But if you recall the couple from my workshop with the problem of the husband's pension, fixed payments for life aren't always what they seem.

Income riders like this always have an extra fee associated with them, typically an additional 1 or 2 percent. When I see variable annuities with this rider, typically the client is paying a total of about 7 percent in fees. What they don't tell you is when you activate the income rider, all they're doing is paying you back your initial premium first, then, if you live long enough, they tap into the interest you earned over the lifetime of the contract.

The other problem I have with income riders is that once you tap into the rider, your lump sum value is no longer accessible to you. If you ever needed a little extra padding, you don't have access to your money anymore. And if you don't choose the right term, if you die before your money can be paid back, your beneficiaries often don't get any death benefit. This is why I strongly, strongly urge against income riders.

Income riders are not exclusive to variable annuities, either. Even fixed annuities and indexed annuities can offer these additions. If a representative has sold you a policy like this or is trying to now, I urge you to walk away and see me for a second opinion.

So, what exactly is the solution to stretching your money over all your years? Choosing the right products to secure and protect your money while it still grows is vital. Income riders are certainly not the answer.

I never use income riders or products with fees and risks. Instead, I utilize indexed annuities with no fees and no risk of loss. I always make sure my clients have access to their entire account balance because you never know when there may be an emergency and a little extra cash is needed.

The performance of the indexed annuities I use has varied over the years. During a down-market year, the returns have been minimal. And during years of market growth, I had a client make 49 percent in one year. I've had years where all my clients average around 20 percent. But I don't like to overpromise, so I usually tell people to expect a steady 4 to 6 percent return over the term of the fixed annuity.

> **When clients ask me how they can create an income stream they can never outlive, I tell them to adhere to the *5 Percent Solution.***

Our *5 Percent Solution* means that you're only taking 5 percent per year from your retirement accounts in any given year. The premise is that if you're only taking 5 percent, but your accounts are making, say, 6 to 7 percent each year, you're never going to run out of money. Most of my clients who follow this rule, in fact, don't even touch the principal of their account since they're seeing about 6 percent growth and are only taking out 5 percent.

If starting today your money never made another penny, you would be able to stretch that money out twenty years by withdrawing 5 percent annually. It is just very basic math. This example may not provide you with a lavish lifestyle, but you will not be destitute or without funds. And of course, your money is going to grow in the next twenty years. I estimate that out of twenty years, your accounts will grow in value for a minimum of fourteen of those years. The account growth coupled with modest withdrawals will help you beat inflation and you will not outlive your money.

Whether you have $30,000, $800,000, or several million dollars in assets, we tell everybody to withdraw in this measured way. It's all about living within your means.

Now, what if you are smart, live well within the means your 5 percent provides, and are fortunate enough to have rising gains on your principal? You have excess money! While leaving a legacy is not always about leaving cash to one or more beneficiaries, let's look now at some tax-efficient options open to you for this excess cash.

If you find that your Required Minimum Distributions alone are too much for you to spend, you could consider what's called a *Qualified Charitable Distribution (QCD)*. A QCD is when you donate all or a portion of your annual required distribution amount from your IRAs to a charity. Since IRA distributions are typically taxable, donating the distribution to charity through this qualified means will make any amount donated completely tax deductible. Reducing your taxable income has many benefits; the main one is your Social Security income may be taxed at a lesser rate!

QCDs only apply when you let the company holding your IRA know how to distribute the funds. You cannot receive your distribution as normal and then donate it. The donation must go directly from your IRA to the charity. At tax time, you will typically receive documentation from both the charity and your IRA supporting the QCD. Be sure your tax account has that information so your return and deduction can be properly processed.

If you don't want to consider a QCD, but still want the tax savings, contributing to a *529 Education Plan* is an excellent alternative. While 529 Plans have many advantages, the main one is tax-free dollars used for future education. There are two types of 529 Plans: the prepaid tuition plan and a savings plan. According to the Consumer Finance Protection Bureau, "Prepaid tuition plans allow families to pay tuition ahead of time for specific colleges or college systems at today's tuition rates."[5] This means that by contributing to a Pennsylvania Prepaid 529 Plan today, your beneficiary can go to college at today's prices in eighteen years. And if the recipient chooses an out-of-state school, the money can be transferred for out-of-state use, but you typically will have to pay at the future tuition price in that case.

---

5   "What are the differences between 529 plans?", Consumer Finance Protection Bureau, June 23, 2021, https://www.consumerfinance.gov/ask-cfpb/what-are-the-differences-between-529-plans-en-2078/.

The second type of 529 is a savings plan for investing your money in mutual funds and stocks to grow over time. You can purchase and manage these plans yourself, or you can also buy them through an advisor. If you purchase through an advisor, there is certainly going to be a management fee, which can be quite steep. I generally do not recommend using the savings plan option, since it's riskier.

529 Plans are a great investment because the money can be used for qualified education expenses at almost any educational institution, including K-12 tuition costs.

TYPE OF EXPENSE	IS IT A QUALIFIED EDUCATION EXPENSE?
Tuition and fees	Yes, up to the full amount of college or vocational school tuition and required fees. Limited to $10,000 per year for K-12.
Books and supplies	For college expenses only
Computers, software, and internet access	For college expenses only
Room and board	For college expenses only, if the student is enrolled at least half-time
Special needs equipment	For college expenses only

TYPE OF EXPENSE	IS IT A QUALIFIED EDUCATION EXPENSE?
Transportation and travel costs	No, costs associated with transportation to and from campus, such as airfare or gas, are not qualified education expenses.
Health insurance	No, even health insurance policies offered by a school are not considered qualified education expenses.
College application and testing fees	No
Extracurricular activity fees	No
Student loans	Yes, with a lifetime limit of $10,000

Source: https://www.savingforcollege.com/article/what-you-can-pay-for-with-a-529-plan

In Pennsylvania, all contributions to a 529 Plan are fully state tax deductible up to the $16,000 IRS gifting limit (per current 2022 law) per donor, per beneficiary. If you really had the excess funds, you could theoretically contribute $16,000 to three children in one year, reducing your taxable state income by $48,000. A married couple can contribute a combined $32,000 per beneficiary, so the savings options are practically limitless. You can also make a one-time contribution of $80,000 ($160,000 for a married couple) and treat that as if you had spread it over the last five years. This is another way to provide an inheritance for your family and take advantage of great tax savings.

QCDs and 529 Plan contributions are just two ways to take advantage of tax savings when you have excess cash, but there are many other options available to you as well. I'd be happy to discuss these options further with you.

> **It doesn't matter what your asset level is, it's important to know how to maximize your retirement savings and ensure it's going to last you a lifetime.**

I talked about both the *5 Percent Solution* and how to utilize excess cash in a tax-advantageous way in this chapter because they go hand-in-hand. By taking advantage of the tax savings, you're adding more money to your pocket each month by reducing your tax bill. And if you take extra money you're saving and invest it, you can continue to compound your money for future use.

CHAPTER 12
IT'S TIME TO TAKE ACTION

We've arrived at the final pages of this book. I really do hope that you take advantage of all the information I've provided you. After all, information is useless without action. Knowledge when acted upon is powerful!

I understand the business I am in. I am in the people business—and I love it! I am in the business of serving people seeking sound financial advice and solutions that allow them peace of mind throughout their retirement years.

The financial planning industry has come a long way in terms of instating more compliance practices for advisors, but the industry has a long way to go. Being a fiduciary is not a requirement to be a financial advisor, which is why many advisors still practice the *suitable* standard. Although I'm not required to work in the best interest of my clients, I choose to be a fiduciary and promise to work in your best interest. (I can't believe I even have to say it, but it's not just required of all professionals.)

Being a woman in this industry, I know how often we are overlooked. Even as a professional, my male peers often don't see me as an equal. Heck, I even have male clients who think they know better than me. And this is exactly why I set out to write this book. I wanted to be sure my clients, and women especially, know they're not alone in this. A client once told me how much she liked working with me because I explained everything in a way that even she understood. That's one of the greatest compliments I've received from my clients. I'm in this business to help people.

If you feel your concerns are not being heard or taken seriously by your current advisor, it might be time for a switch. And for those of you who are married, if you can't get your spouse to read this book, I encourage you to either join me for a Live Educational Workshop or you can tune into my radio show, *Retirement and Income Radio.*[6]

At the workshop and on the radio, I go over many of the same topics I've talked about in this book. It's a

---

6   https://www.financialadvisorlancaster.com/workshops.html; https://www.financialadvisorlancaster.com/radio.html

great way to get your hesitant spouse, family members, and friends to hear what I have to say.

To encourage you to take those next steps toward building a secure retirement, I invite you to join me for a complimentary consultation in my office. The best way you can set yourself on the right track for retirement is by letting me tailor strategies to suit your needs, and I cannot do that without talking to you one-on-one.

Because you took the opportunity to read this book and evaluate your situation on your own, I know you're the type of person I can help. Maybe you're still nervous about taking that next step. After all, big changes are hard, especially when it feels like they're all happening at once. To ease your mind about calling me and coming in the first time, let me lay out what that first meeting will look like.

When you first step into our lobby, you'll see that Helen's war memorabilia is on display alongside her photo and a synopsis of her story. This memorial pays tribute to her life and serves as a reminder of why I choose to do what I do every day.

The first thing I'll go over with you is your tax returns. Looking over your taxes gives me an excellent picture of your income sources, and since I am a tax expert, this allows me to see where I can find you some tax savings. Then we'll go over all your investment account statements, which I'll carefully read through to point out the hidden fees you're paying, where you're taking on too much risk, and how I can maximize your account performance. If you have life insurance or long-term care policies, I encourage you to bring them too. I'm happy to provide any insight free of charge, so leave your checkbook at home.

The first time we meet will be very casual, and I do not expect you to make a decision that same day. I simply want to present how your current investments may not be serving you well and how you might benefit from my strategies. The first meeting is simply my time to hear all about you. I want to hear your concerns and desires for the future; that's the only way I'll be able to really help you.

Remember, I am not going to charge you any fees, and I'll never offer you a product that will charge you fees. As a fiduciary, it's my responsibility to be transparent with you and give you all the facts; I'm not going to sneak anything in there. There's no such thing as a stupid question. I want you to leave my office feeling satisfied and not as though I didn't listen to or address all of your concerns.

When I have a clear picture of your unique situation, that's when I'm going to develop a personalized plan for you. This plan will include how to maximize your retirement savings by eliminating fees and risk, how to create a lifelong stream of income, and how to maximize your investment returns year after year.

If, like most people, you decide that I can help you and your family, I'll be more than happy to welcome you into my own family. At The Richardson Group, we treat our clients like family. My business is a small, family-owned firm. I personally know all of my clients by name; I've even been to many of their homes. Many clients have my personal cell phone number, so I'm always accessible. My clients know they can always come to me with questions, even if they are not directly related to what I do here.

I see you as an individual with your own set of values and concerns. It's very important to me that you're comfortable with your retirement plans and that you can reasonably reach the goals you have. Looking after your spouse or family after you pass is equally important to me, because I know everyone is someone's family member, like my grandmother Helen was to me.

It's time to act. Give me a call, come into my office, bring all your information along with you, and let's start planning the rest of your life together. Building a secure retirement starts now.

Jordyn invites you to use this certificate to
reserve your FREE financial consultation

VALUE **$600** YOURS
WORTH FREE

CALL TODAY TO RESERVE YOUR TIME
717-394-0840

APPENDIX

ADVANTAGES OF ANNUITIES

Tax-Deferred Growth: The interest earned in your account is not taxed unless touched. Your money grows tax deferred.

Safety: Annuities are among the most guaranteed and secure investments available.

Avoid Probate: Annuities transfer to a beneficiary without the need for probate or a will.

Income: At any time, an annuity can change from a savings or accumulation vehicle to an income vehicle. Annuities can provide an income you cannot outlive.

Estate Planning: Annuities are used in estate planning to help protect assets in the event of a long-term care situation.

Interest Income: Many annuities offer monthly interest payments without ever having to touch your principal.

Death Benefit: In the event of death, beneficiaries have several options for income or lump sum settlement payments.

Fees: No contract fee or sales commissions are deducted from your account value.

Comparison: Interest rates on annuities are usually higher than bank CDs or other fully guaranteed products.

Access: Unlike bank CDs, you have access to the funds during the guarantee period.

DISADVANTAGES OF ANNUITIES

Penalty for Early Withdrawals: During the guarantee period, if you withdraw more than the contract allows, a penalty is applied. Most annuities allow you to withdraw 10 percent of the value, each year, without penalty.

Tax Penalty Prior to Age 59½: Access to annuity funds before age 59½ in any tax-deferred investment may be subject to an additional IRS tax penalty of 10 percent.

ABOUT THE AUTHOR

JORDYN RICHARDSON is a graduate of Pennsylvania State University, where she studied business and Mandarin Chinese. Jordyn's favorite activities include cooking for friends and family, hitting the golf course, skiing, and making pottery.

Upon joining the family business, Jordyn became a certified Medicare agent and a tax expert. Jordyn hosts live seminars, often inviting exclusively women to attend. If you become one of her clients, you'll be invited to join her women's group, which she invites for lunches and other activities. Jordyn also hosts a radio show, *Retirement and Income Radio*. If you need anything notarized, you can even see Jordyn to help you with that! Jordyn has also earned the Federal Retirement Consultant designation; if you or a loved one are a federal employee needing help understanding your FERS pension, TSP, or group life insurance, Jordyn is your go-to!

She is a great believer in lifelong learning for herself and her clients. She knows that understanding the financial options available is only a matter of clear explanations. Jordyn has educated thousands of seniors on how to secure their retirement and avoid fees, risk, and spousal poverty. She is a highly sought-after speaker as she brings a unique perspective to the financial world and has even won several awards for excellence in her field.

Jordyn has found her calling in financial planning for women. She is there to make sure you don't have to do it alone.

Printed in Great Britain
by Amazon

44477609R00088